Uncle John's
BATHROOM READER®
CAT LOVER'S
COMPANION

Uncle John's BATHROOM READER®

CAT L●VER'S COMPANION

PORTABLE PRESS

Bathroom Readers' Institute
San Diego, California, and Ashland, Oregon

Uncle John's Bathroom Reader
Cat Lover's Companion

The following are registered trademarks: "Bathroom Reader,"
"Bathroom Readers' Institute," "Portable Press,"
and "Uncle John's Bathroom Reader."

For information, visit us at www.bathroomreader.com, or write to:
Uncle John's Bathroom Reader
Portable Press, 5880 Oberlin Drive, San Diego, CA 92121
e-mail: unclejohn@advmkt.com

Library of Congress Cataloging-in-Publication Data

Uncle John's bathroom reader cat lover's companion.
p. cm.
ISBN-13: 978-1-59223-687-9 (hardcover)
ISBN-10: 1-59223-687-1 (hardcover)
1. Cats--Miscellanea. 2. Cats--Humor. I. Title: Bathroom reader
cat lover's companion. II. Title: Cat lover's companion.
SF445.5.U53 2006
636.8--dc22

2006016488

Printed in Canada

06 07 08 09 10   10 9 8 7 6 5 4 3 2 1

Project Team

Gordon Javna, Editor-in-Chief
JoAnn Padgett, Director, Editorial and Production
Melinda Allman, Developmental Editor
Jennifer Payne, Production Editor / Contributor
Jennifer Thornton, Managing Editor
Connie Vazquez, Product Manager

Thank You!

The Bathroom Readers' Hysterical Society sincerely
thanks the following additional people whose advice
and assistance made this book possible.

Sydney Stanley
Amy Miller
Michael Brunsfeld
Karen J. Fisher
Allen Orso
Julia Papps
Barb Porsche
Tamar Schwartz
Woody Young
Laurel, Mana, Dylan, and Chandra
Friesens
Raincoast Books
Michelle Sedgwick
Our Families
Sophie, Liz, and Wiggs Dannyboy

Thank You Contributors!

We sincerely thank the following people who contributed selections to this work.

Toney Allman
Myles Callum
Jamuna Carroll
Jenness I. Crawford
Jacqueline Damian
Padraic Duffy
Christina Factor
Debbie K. Hardin
Lise Jorgensen
Andy Levy-Ajzenkopf
Art Montague
Ryan Murphy
Diana Moes VandeHoef

Contents

Caring for Kitty

Histori-cats

Mixed Bag

Our Heroes

Puzzles and Quizzes

Introduction

Here at the Bathroom Readers' Institute, we love animals—dogs, elephants, badgers, hamsters, even skunks—but especially cats. So it was a no-brainer to fill this book with our favorite cat tales. From Persians to Wegies, longhairs to lions, advertising icons to stars of stage and screen, they're all here.

We also found answers to some pressing cat-cerns:

- In what European city do stray cats get a free lunch?
- What's the most common cat blood type?
- Why do cats always land on their feet?
- What is my cat trying to communicate with her whiskers?
- How many tickets did the musical *Cats* sell during its years on Broadway?
- Who created cartoon icons like Garfield, Hobbes, and Felix?
- What cat holds the record for having the most toes? Catching the most mice?
- How can I tell if my kitty's allergic to me?
- Which cats had a wedding, and how much did it cost?

Along the way, we uncovered the origins of some of our favorite cat phrases: Did you know "there's more than one way to skin a cat" has nothing to do with cats, and "playing cat and mouse" originated with suffragettes in early 20th-century England? We learned about legendary cat lovers including Edgar Allan Poe, Charles Dickens, and Theodore Roosevelt, all of whom doted on their feline friends. And we uncovered efforts around the country to rescue and protect endangered lions, tigers, leopards, and other wild cats.

So sit back, relax, and give your favorite feline a scratch. *Uncle John's Bathroom Reader Cat Lover's Companion* was made just for you.

As always, go with the flow . . .

The Staff of the
Bathroom Readers' Institute

Wonderful Whisker Power

*A cat's whiskers aren't just beautiful; they're a marvel
of form and function. Here are 10 things you probably
didn't know about your cat's whiskers.*

1. The scientific name for whiskers is *vibrissae*, and they're
specialized sensory organs on a cat's body (mostly on his
cheeks). On average, cats have 24 cheek whiskers—12
on each side of their face—that are arranged in four
horizontal rows.

2. Each whisker is double the thickness of an ordinary hair
and is rooted in the cat's upper lip. Every root connects to
200 or more nerve endings under kitty's skin that transmit
information directly to his brain.

3. Cats use their whiskers to gain information about their
environment. They can avoid bushes, sofas, and other
obstacles with whisker power alone. Air currents create a
tiny breeze as they move around an object. Cats feel this
change with their whiskers and avoid objects in their
path.

4. Whiskers direct hunting cats to a successful pounce.
In one experiment, a blindfolded cat was placed in an

enclosure with a live mouse. When the cat's whiskers touched the mouse, the cat grabbed his prey and delivered a killing bite in one-tenth of a second.

5. Once the prey is in the cat's mouth, muscles in his face allow the whiskers to curl forward and sense any movement that might mean the animal is still alive and possibly dangerous. Also, when cats crouch over an intended meal, they wrap their whiskers around the prey to make sure the animal is truly dead and safe to eat.

6. The width of a cat's outstretched whiskers is usually the same as the width of his body. So cats use their whiskers to measure the diameter of holes or other openings to make sure they're wide enough to enter without being trapped. When kitty overeats and gains too much weight, though, his whiskers stay the same size. So a fat cat may misjudge the size of his body and get stuck in a hole—one good reason not to overdo the treats.

7. Cheeks are the most well-known spots for whiskers, but cats also have them on the backs of their two front paws. These whiskers are shorter than the ones on a cat's cheeks and they help him walk over uneven ground without

stumbling. Paw whiskers also help cats determine the size and position of captured prey.

8. Cats have whiskers over their eyes and on their chins, too. These are responsive to touch, but they aren't as important to a cat's survival as the cheek and paw whiskers are.

9. A cat's whiskers should never be trimmed because without his whiskers to guide him, a cat can get disoriented in the dark.

10. Whiskers are such an important part of a cat's physiology that the feline fetus develops whiskers before any other hairs. And when kittens are born, they're blind and deaf, but the touch sensors on their whiskers are fully operational.

* * *

The Language of Whiskers

Whiskers can also be used to communicate. Here are some tips for deciphering what your cat's whiskers are saying:

- A calm, resting, or friendly cat holds his whiskers out to the sides.
- An alert, curious, or excited cat's whiskers point upward.
- Backward-pointing whiskers often indicate that a cat feels defensive or is angry. So, you . . . human . . . the one with the kitty shampoo and bath supplies in hand: back off!

How to Lose a Cat Show

Come on . . . anyone can win a cat show. Fabulous felines do it every year. Here are six easy steps guaranteed to keep you out of the winner's circle of any of the Cat Fanciers' Association (CFA) shows around the country.

1. Don't register.

To win a cat show, felines must be registered with the organization sponsoring the event. The animal's name, breed, lineage, sex, and age have to be documented, and sponsors require that owners provide proof their cats have been fixed and have had their vaccinations. If you show up without any notice; they probably won't even let you in.

2. Let Fluffy run wild.

CFA show rules require that kitties be caged at all times. If you let your cat have the run of the showroom, you'll definitely attract negative attention.

3. Keep grooming to a minimum.

Or better yet, don't do it at all. There aren't written rules about grooming at cat shows, but any successful exhibitor knows that show cats ought to get a shampoo, pedicure, and teeth cleaning before the event. Even cat handlers dress tastefully if they want to win; many coordinate their attire to match their cats. If you're determined to lose, letting your cat arrive at the show with matted fur and ragged nails should do the trick.

4. Teach Fluffy to bite.

Judges tend to prefer cats who are docile and easy to handle, so train your cat to bite, scratch, and squirm, and you'll be sure not to win.

5. Talk to the judges.

Cat show judging is mostly subjective, and rules usually prohibit conversation between exhibitors and judges. So lobby the judges with zeal, perhaps offer them a cocktail from your cooler. There's a good chance you'll be disqualified.

6. Bring in a cheering section.

Cat shows, like tennis matches and chess games, are solemn events. Polite clapping is permitted, but more enthusiastic responses are frowned upon. To ensure that your cat goes home empty-pawed, enlist the help of your most raucous family and friends. Ask them to wear colored wigs and carry banners. They should cheer, boo, and even try to get a round of the wave going. Any of these behaviors will offend the judges.

Courageous Cats

*Here are some feline rescue missions that are so
amazing you'll find them hard to believe.*

Speed Dial 911

When Tommy, an orange-and-tan striped cat, saw his
wheelchair-bound owner sprawled out on the floor near
his bed, the cat dialed 911 for help. Sound unlikely?
Possibly. Unless you consider that Tommy's owner, Gary
Rosheisen of Columbus, Ohio, had trained the cat to dial
911 in just such an emergency. Rosheisen could never tell
whether or not Tommy was picking up on the unusual
training, but he kept the phone on the living room floor
and programmed the emergency number into speed dial,
just in case.

In January 2006, police got a call from Rosheisen's
apartment. No one responded when they answered, so
concerned officers went to the apartment to investigate.
When they arrived, they found Tommy lying near the
phone and Rosheisen in the bedroom. No one can say for
sure, of course, if the cat dialed for help, but the police
can't explain the call any other way. Rosheisen, who
recovered from his fall, has no doubt about Tommy, however. "He's my hero," Rosheisen says.

Won't You Be My Neighbor

Many neighborhoods have a watch program, but few boast one whose primary watchdog is a cat. In the small Scottish community of Kirkwall, Smudge is the town hero. In the space of just two weeks, he alerted his neighborhood to two emergencies.

- The first involved an elderly woman who injured herself in a fall. Smudge returned to the woman's home again and again, drawing attention to the house. Neighbors finally checked on the woman, discovered her injury, and called the police.
- Days later, Smudge repeatedly pushed at the kitchen door of his own home, insisting to go out. When his owner, Willie Garriock, finally let Smudge outside, the cat ran in the direction of a fire alarm going off down the street. Willie followed Smudge and helped the elderly man who lived there escape. Says Garriock, "I am sure everyone on the street feels a lot safer with Smudge watching out for them."

Preventing a Cat-astrophe

An unidentified cat made international news in April 2006, when it was credited with saving an abandoned newborn baby in Cologne, Germany. The cat meowed loudly on the doorstep of the home where the baby had been abandoned. When the occupants came outside to see what the ruckus was about, they found the child. Police say the boy would have suffered from hypothermia and might have died if he had remained outside all night. But thanks to the cat's heroic efforts, he was fine.

* * *

Family Ties

A Pennsylvania puppy rejected by its canine mother found a new family in April 2006. A two-year-old striped cat named Zoey adopted the puppy as part of her brood of new kittens. The puppy, who was the runt of his litter, was about the same size as Zoey's kittens, and at feeding time, he lined up with his feline brothers and sisters for some of Mother's milk.

The Ten Cat-mandments

1. I am Lord of the house.

2. Thou shall have no other pets before me.

3. Thou shall never ignore me.

4. I shall ignore thee whenever I choose.

5. Thou shall be grateful that I give thee the time of day.

6. Thou shall remember my food dish and keep it full.

7. Thou shall provide abundant toys and treats for me.

8. Thou shall always have a lap ready for me to curl up in.

9. Thou shall shower me with attention.

10. Above all, thou shall do anything it takes to keep me happy.

TV Tabbies

Test your television feline IQ: match each cat to its description.

1. Toonces
2. Mrs. Whiskerson
3. Snowball II
4. Mr. Henderson

5. Fluffy
6. Ling Ling
7. Henrietta Pussycat
8. Salem

A. *Friends* character Rachel Green adopted this hairless sphynx cat because it reminded her of her grandmother's pet. However, Rachel soon discovered the cat had a nasty disposition and sold it to Central Perk barista Gunther.

B. This cat belonging to *Saturday Night Live*'s Lyle and Brenda Clark (made famous by actors Dana Carvey and Victoria Jackson) got behind the wheel of the family car whenever he had the chance—and generally drove over a cliff. The character was the brainchild of Steve Martin, who played Lyle in the first episode.

C. It was a beautiful day in the neighborhood when this timid, girlish cat, who lived in a tree on *Mr. Rogers' Neighborhood*, put on a frilly dress and a pretty hat and came out to meet the neighbors. Fred Rogers was the puppeteer behind this character.

D. *The Brady Bunch* house may have been a groovy place for kids during the late 1960s and early 1970s, but it wasn't pet-friendly. The family cat appeared only in the first episode. And Tiger, the family dog, disappeared without a clear explanation after the second season.

E. Using magic to help when her mortal husband, Darrin, couldn't find the right model to star in his latest ad campaign, *Bewitched*'s Samantha twitched her nose and turned this Siamese cat into a young woman. Samantha eventually twitched the woman back into a cat—but not before the Stevens' nosy neighbor, Gladys Kravitz, caught the model drinking milk out of a pet bowl.

F. All TV witches should have cats, right? The young witch in *Sabrina, the Teenage Witch* is no exception. But this smart-mouthed talking cat was actually a man put under a spell for 100 years as punishment for trying to take over the world.

G. The second in a string of felines belonging to *The Simpsons*, this black cat saved patriarch Homer from a burning treehouse. The animal also cuddled up to Santa's Little Helper (the family dog) when no one was watching.

H. Bachelorette Sally Rogers on *The Dick Van Dyke Show* may not have gotten a lot of dates, but she always had this male feline to come home to.

For answers, turn to page 220.

Jokes on Us, Part 1

*Moan, groan, and laugh along with some
of our favorite (bad) cat jokes.*

Where do single cats advertise for a date?
The purr-sonal ads

What do cats like to eat for dessert?
Mice cream

What cats make good bowlers?
Alley cats

What movie is a feline favorite?
The Sound of Mew-sic

Why was the kitten in such a bad mood?
She needed a catnap.

What game do cats love to play with
mice?
Catch

For more jokes, turn to page 81.

Maine Coons and Wegies

*Two of the world's oldest breeds,
these cats have legendary histories.*

Ask an owner of a Maine coon how this breed got started, and you'll get a variety of answers. These gentle kitties are the subjects of numerous stories, and it's sometimes difficult to separate fact from fiction.

Theory #1: They're a crossbreed.
According to legend, the first Maine coon was born when a cat mated with a raccoon. Yes, Maine coons generally have long hair and brown coats with dark tabby stripes, akin to the fur of a raccoon, but such intra-species breeding is biologically impossible.

Theory #2: Early colonists mated domestic cats with American bobcats.
The Maine coon's tufted ears, tufted toes, and long bushy tails do resemble the bobcat's, but this theory is also unlikely because wild animals rarely mate with domestic creatures.

Theory #3: Marie Antoinette's expatri-cats formed the foundation of the breed.

During the late 18th century, a revolution broke out in France, and Queen Marie Antoinette was headed for the chopping block. In preparation for an escape, she supposedly loaded her six pampered, purebred, long-haired cats onto a sailing ship headed for Maine. (Why Maine, you ask? No one seems to know.) Before Marie could join her cats at the docks, though, revolutionaries captured (and ultimately beheaded) her. So the cats had to continue the journey without her. They landed in Maine, broke free, mated with American domestic cats, and formed a new breed: the Maine coon.

Theory #4: They're a hybrid.

A more likely story is that American shorthairs mated with the Persian and Turkish Angora cats sailors brought from Europe and created the Maine coon.

Rediscover Me

No matter their origin, there's no doubt that Maine

coons were prized in early America. Maine coons are considered to be one of the most intelligent, amiable breeds around, and they're skilled mousers. By the 1860s, farmers were showing off their Maine coons at the Skowhegan Fair in Maine, one of the first recorded cat shows in the United States. And in 1895, a brown tabby Maine coon named Cosey won the first U.S. cat show held at Madison Square Garden in New York City.

By the early 20th century, imported Persians, Turkish Angoras, and other exotic longhairs had become popular in the United States, and Maine coons were all but abandoned; the breed was even declared nearly extinct during the late 1950s. But active breeding programs in the 1960s and 1970s brought the Maine coon back, and today this kitty is again one of the most popular breeds in the United States.

Too Big for Thor to Handle

When it comes to legends, the Maine coon has a lot in common with another breed that hails from a similarly harsh environment: the Norwegian forest cat (called a "Wegie" for short and *skogkatt* in Norwegian). Relatively new to the United States, this cat is centuries old in its native Scandinavia and even plays a role in Norse mythology. According to legend, giant *skogkatts*, who were too big for even Thor (the mighty Norse god of thunder) to lift, pulled the carriage of the love goddess Freya. And a collection of Scandinavian folk and fairy tales called

Popular Tales from the Norse (published in 1859) is replete with references to huge and furry cats.

The real origin of this strong, stocky breed remains unknown, but many people suspect that the Norwegian forest cats may have migrated to Scandinavia from southern Europe. They may also be descendants of long-haired cats brought home during the Middle Ages by European crusaders returning from treks to Asia and the Middle East.

Coming to America

It wasn't until 1979 that the first Wegie breeding pair arrived in the United States. They quickly became popular with  cat lovers because they are smart, alert, friendly, and playful (indeed, some owners say their Wegies are obsessed with toys). Late to mature, these cats remain kittenish for as many as four to five years. Norwegian forest cats are also a quiet breed. They don't vocalize much, but when they do, they use a variety of chirps and trills, rather than the standard meow.

To read more about breeds, turn to page 51.

Pugilistic Pusses

*If you're wondering what cats and early movie making have
to do with each other, bear with us. One of America's first motion
pictures involved a ring, a trainer, two boxing cats, and the
man best known for helping us all see the light.*

Thomas Alva Edison was one of the fathers of modern
movie making. In 1888, Edison started tinkering with
a movie camera that would, he said, "do for the eye what
the phonograph does for the ear." Edison wanted to create
a single motion picture camera that could record succes-
sive action (other movie cameras predate Edison's, but
these could not record an entire series of action alone;
more than one camera was required).

By 1891, Edison and several associates had created the
Kinetoscope. This wooden contraption acted as both a
camera and the peep-show-type implement that allowed
people to see the movie. Viewers peered into a lens
mounted on top of the Kinetoscope to watch the film.

The Black Maria
With the camera ready for use, all Edison needed was a
place to film his movies. There were no soundstages back
then, so he invented one. Edison consulted with photographers and other inventors to create a building he called

the Black Maria (pronounced "Mariah") in West Orange, New Jersey. The studio was so named because it resembled a late 19th-century police car ("black Maria" is old slang for a paddy wagon). The studio was boxy and painted black inside and out. Its ceiling was actually a large window that could be opened to allow in sunlight; early cameras needed bright sunlight to work properly. The entire building was also mounted on a large revolving pivot so that filmmakers could rotate it to follow the sun as it moved across the horizon.

The first movie Edison and his assistants made in the Black Maria was called *Fred Ott's Sneeze*. It was a silent dramatic rendering of an embellished and comical sneeze

as performed by Edison employee Fred Ott. Ultimately, Edison and his associates made dozens of movies in the Black Maria from 1892, when it opened, to 1901, when it closed and Edison moved his movie-making studio to New York City.

Punchy Kitties

Here's where the cats come in. Vaudeville showman Henry Welton had a circus of trained cats that he toured around New York City during the 1890s. His cats rode bicycles and performed somersaults; some even walked through fire.

For the 1894 30-second movie *Boxing Cats* (filmed in the Black Maria), Welton chose two of his kitties, dressed them in boxing gear (including gloves and shorts), and set them up in a miniature ring. The cats weren't really fighting—at least not the way cats would fight outside the ring. Instead, they looked more like humans, standing up on two legs and sparring with gloves on their front paws. Welton also appeared the film; he supervised the sparring match and helped keep the cats standing upright.

Boxing Cats and other Edison movies fell out of favor during the early 1900s as motion picture projectors were perfected and movies as we know them came into vogue. People no longer had to peer into a box to watch a 30-second film. But Edison's early foray into movies remains a progenitor of the modern filmmaking era.

Cat Stats
By the Numbers

Cats have racked up some incredible statistics.

3

Number of cat blood types: A, B, and AB. Most cats are type A.

5

Number of toes on a normal cat's front paws; back paws have four toes.

10

Percentage of a cat's bones that are in his tail

16

Number of hours a day that a cat spends sleeping

20

Percentage of cats who are left-pawed, meaning they favor that side. Another 40 percent are right pawed, and 40 percent are ambidextrous.

31 mph
Average speed at which a domestic cat can sprint

70 mph
Average speed at which a cheetah (the world's fastest cat) can sprint

95
Percentage of cat owners who talk to their cats

100+
Number of different vocal sounds a cat can make. Dogs make about 10.

102 degrees Fahrenheit
A cat's normal body temperature

230
Average number of bones in an adult cat's body. Adult humans have 206.

420
Record number of kittens born to one mother cat; the tabby's name was Dusty, and she hailed from Texas.

500,000

Cats enlisted by British forces to act as mousers in World War I trenches. The British also used cats as mousers during World War II; the animals patrolled military food stores. In fact, the Brits thought the feline force so important to the 1940s war effort that the kitties had their own powdered milk rations.

500 million

Number of domestic cats worldwide. In the United States alone, there are about 53 million.

$2 billion+

Amount of money American cat owners spend annually on cat food

*   *   *

A group of kittens is called a "kindle." A group of adult cats is called a "clowder."

*   *   *

> "Cats are kindly masters, just so long as you remember your place."
> —*Paul Gray, author*

On the Strip, Part 1

*Cats have entertained us in comic strips for
nearly 100 years. Here are some of our favorites.*

Krazy Kat

George Herriman got his first cartooning job in 1897 as an
illustrator for the *Los Angeles Herald*. Over the next 13
years, he illustrated and wrote several comic strips for that
newspaper. One of them, called *The Dingbat Family*, simul-
taneously told the story of a human family and of a cat
and mouse cavorting beneath the floorboards of the family's home.

Krazy Kat and Ignatz Mouse were those animals, and in
1913, Herriman gave them their own black-and-white
comic strip. The stories most often revolved around Krazy
Kat's unrequited love for Ignatz. The mouse threw bricks
at Krazy Kat, a gesture the kitty mistook as a sign of affection, and the cartoon's third character, a police dog named
Officer Pupp, tried repeatedly to jail Ignatz for the brick
throwing.

The mainstream public wasn't enthusiastic about *Krazy
Kat*, but intellectuals loved it—James Joyce and e. e. cum-
mings were fans. And William Randolph Hearst, who
owned and published more than two dozen newspapers,

liked the cartoon so much that he gave Herriman a life-time contract to print them. Hearst also produced several animated *Krazy Kat* shorts during the early 1900s.

The strip, which *Comics Journal* called the number one comic of the 20th century, made its full-color debut in 1935 and ran until Herriman died in 1944. In all, he wrote and drew more than 3,000 *Krazy Kat* cartoons.

Krazy Kat Fact: Michael Stipe of the band REM has a tatoo of Krazy Kat and Ignatz.

Felix the Cat

Before Mickey Mouse, Donald Duck, Porky Pig, and Bugs Bunny, Felix the Cat reigned as king of the animated animals. In 1919, Felix got his first gig on the big screen. By 1923, he had a string of short silent movies to his credit and also had his own syndicated comic strip. And in 1928, Felix was part of the very first television broadcast.

The wide-eyed, grinning black-and-white cat was the creation of New Jersey cartoonist Otto Messmer. Messmer first drew Felix in 1919 when a film producer acquaintance asked him to create a quick animated short to fill in for another animator. Thus, Felix the Cat was born. In that first film, *Feline Follies*, Felix was called Master Tom, and the cartoon was so successful with the public that Paramount, the studio financing the operation, ordered an entire series. By the third installment, Tom had become Felix.

For the next few years, Felix starred in several films and

comic strips. He was a unique animal character because he wasn't bumbling. Instead, he was a clever, mischievous hero who used wit and ingenuity to solve problems. He was also funny. In one installment, Messmer spoofed Hollywood by having Felix be the pet of an out-of-work actor. During the course of the story, Felix met up with Gloria Swanson, saved Douglas Fairbanks from a swarm of mosquitoes, and was signed to a studio contract by Cecil B. DeMille.

Felix's movie career stalled as talking films replaced silent pictures. Messmer and his team were unable to turn Felix into a talkie star, and during the 1930s, Walt Disney's Mickey Mouse took over Felix's place as America's premier animated animal. But the cat stayed alive in comic strips that ran in newspapers around the country. And in the 1950s, he returned to television.

Felix Fact: During the 1930s, Pat Sullivan, one of the producers with whom Messmer worked in the early days, took credit for creating *Felix the Cat*. He even went so far as to claim that his wife once brought home a stray who was the inspiration for Felix. But when Felix found new life on television, producers of the cartoons made sure to credit Messmer with the character's creation.

To read more about popular cartoon cats, turn to page 45.

Broadway *Cats*
By the Numbers

*"Now and Forever," proclaimed the advertising slogan
for Cats. With a record-breaking run on Broadway, Andrew
Lloyd Webber's feline revue based on a book of poems by
T. S. Eliot seems to have meant that literally.*

1

Actress who stayed with *Cats* during its entire Broadway run. Marlene Danielle began in the chorus and worked her way up to a major player, ultimately portraying the sassy female feline Bombalurina.

11

Tony nominations earned in 1983. *Cats* won seven of those, including Best Musical and a nod to the late T. S. Eliot for the lyrics.

18

Years *Cats* spent on Broadway. The show opened in 1982 and closed in 2000. On June 19, 1997, *Cats* became the longest-running show on Broadway, a title it held until 2006, when another Webber musical, *Phantom of the Opera*, surpassed it.

35

Major cat characters in the musical,
including Grizabela, Rum Tum Tugger, and Old
Deuteronomy

150+

Times the musical's signature tune, "Memory," has been
recorded. Barbra Streisand, Barry Manilow, and others have
all put their own stamp on the song.

200+

Actors who portrayed the cats over the years

1939

The year T. S. Eliot published *Old Possum's Book of
Practical Cats*. Forty years later, composer Andrew Lloyd
Webber set this book of poems to music to create *Cats*.
Eliot died in 1965, so Webber approached the writer's
widow, Valerie, for permission to use the poems in the
musical. Valerie Eliot gave Webber the rights on one condition: he couldn't rewrite a word. So *Cats* became a series
of vignettes, each featuring one of the poems.

3,000

Pounds of yak hair used over the years to make the cats' wigs

7,485

Performances on Broadway. The show also had 8,945 performances at London's West End.

25,000

Makeup brushes used during the show's Broadway run

$250,000

First-day ticket sales for the Broadway premiere. In the first 50 minutes alone, ticket sales reached $50,000.

1 million

Pounds of dry ice used for smoke

8 million

Tickets sold for *Cats* during its 18-year Broadway run

* * *

The cats in *Cats* are called Jellicles, even though the show never really explains what that means. The term comes from the Old Possum himself—it's a corruption of the phrase "dear little cat," as spoken by T. S. Eliot's young niece.

A Seaworthy Tale

This cat just wouldn't go down with his ships.

During World War II, a black cat named Oscar took to the high seas as the mascot for the German battleship *Bismarck*. But Oscar wasn't a particularly lucky mascot. Instead, he sailed on three ships hit by torpedoes.

Oscar Ahoy!

The *Bismarck* sank on May 27, 1941, when a British destroyer called the *Cossack* launched a torpedo and took down the German vessel. When the *Cossack*'s men searched the wreckage for survivors, they found Oscar alive and sitting on a piece of floating debris. The sailors rescued the cat, renamed him Unsinkable Sam, and adopted him as their own.

Oscar sailed with the *Cossack* for five months before it was sunk by a German U-boat. When the British aircraft carrier *Ark Royal* arrived at the site after the attack, the sailors made an amazing discovery: there was Oscar . . . alive and well on the debris and awaiting rescue. The *Ark Royal*'s seamen brought Oscar on board, fed him, and, like the *Cossack* sailors before them, adopted him as their own.

On Dry Land

Three weeks later, though, Oscar found himself in the water again. A German submarine torpedoed the *Ark Royal* off the coast of Gibraltar and sank the ship. Once again, Oscar the cat was found among the wreckage.

This proved too much for the British Royal Navy, and superstition got the best of the sailors. After all, the black cat had sailed on three ships, and all had sunk. He needed to lose his sea legs before the British lost any more ships.

So the sailors brought Oscar back to the United Kingdom and sent him to a retirement home for sailors in Ireland. Official military reports read, "Oscar, the *Bismarck*'s cat, finished his days at the Home for Sailors in Belfast." There he lived until his death in 1955.

* * *

"People that hate cats will come back as mice in their next life."

—*Faith Resnick, author*

Hey! Why's She Doing That?

Many cat owners often wonder why their cats behave the way they do. Luckily for them, we've got the skinny on some of cats' most common behaviors.

Why do cats lick their fur after being petted?

This is a cat's way of tasting and getting to know you. Cats' sense of taste is better developed than their sense of sight. By relying on taste instead of sight alone, your kitty is making a detailed mental picture of you so she can remember whom to hit up for a treat or chin scratch later on.

If a cat lies on her back, does this mean I should scratch her tummy?

This varies from cat to cat. Some kitties love to have their stomachs petted, but others detest it. A cat lying with her stomach and chest exposed is happy and at ease, and the behavior shows trust and comfort with whoever is present. So go ahead—scratch her belly. But if she nips at you, don't try it again.

Why do cats salivate when they are happy (especially when they're being petted and are purring)?

Young nursing kittens associate contentment with food. Later in life, when cats are happy, they salivate because being content reminds them of food.

When a cat's blinking slows down, is he tired?

Cats are tired most of the time—it's exhausting being pampered! But slow blinking just means your cat is relaxed. She may or may not take a nap—it probably depends on how much attention you're willing to give her at that moment.

If my cat rubs her whole body against me, does she want my attention?

Probably. But she's also marking you as her own. Cats have scent glands around their mouths. When she rubs against you, she leaves behind some of her scent to ward off other felines who might try to claim you as theirs.

The Klock's Meow

You know him: a round head, moving eyes and tail, and a goofy grin. Black and white Kit-Cat Klocks have been hanging on walls in homes and businesses all over the United States since the Great Depression. But do you know the whole story?

Today, Woody Young, owner of the California Clock Company in Fountain Valley, California, makes the Kit-Cat Klocks. Located in nearby Torrance, the factory churns out dozens of clocks a day for sale around the United States. And despite rising costs and stagnant prices (the last time Kit-Cats saw their sticker price rise was in 1994), Young is determined to keep Kit-Cat's manufacture in the United States because, he says, "It's an American icon."

It's Always the Mouse

Kit-Cat Klocks first made their way into American homes during the 1930s. And although the details have been lost over time, here's how Young thinks it all got started.

In 1932, Clifford Stone, a manufacturer in Portland, Oregon, made the first Kit-Cat Klock. He credited another man, Earl Arnalalt, with the design, but it's unclear how the two knew each other.

How Arnalalt came up with the idea for the clock is

also unknown. Many people believe that Kit-Cat's inspiration was Felix the Cat, an early 20th-century cartoon kitty. But Young calls that a common misconception; the only thing those two characters share is the fact that they're both black-and-white cats. Instead, Young and others connected to Kit-Cat believe that Arnalalt got his inspiration from America's most famous cartoon character.

They speculate that Arnalalt once worked for the Walt Disney Company and that he turned Disney's Mickey Mouse into the cat clock. In fact, the templates for the Kit-Cat design and for early Mickey Mouse drawings are similar; says Young, "Only the ears are different."

No matter the origin, Americans responded to Kit-Cat almost immediately. The clocks were mechanical back then—you needed to wind them with a key—and they sold for just a couple of dollars. Even that small amount was hard earned during the Depression, but Americans shelled out the bucks nonetheless because Kit-Cat made them smile.

Leading the Way

In the 1940s, Clifford Stone moved his manufacturing plant from Oregon to Seattle, Washington. He also renamed it "Allied Manufacturing," an homage to the American presence in World War II. Allied Manufacturing did its part to support the war effort by providing materials for Boeing and by researching innovations in mechanical design. One discovery propelled them to the forefront of the clock-making business.

In the mid-1940s, engineers at Allied pioneered electric clock motors. These new designs made most wind-up clocks obsolete. Stone and his crew put small electric motors into Kit-Cat, and sales took off. By the 1950s, the black-and-white kitty had become the best-selling clock in the United States. It cost just $3.95 and was popular with both the general public and the Hollywood elite. Many movie stars were fans, and Lucille Ball was one of the biggest. She bought Kit-Cat Klocks by the dozens to give as gifts.

Around this time, a woman whose husband worked for Allied began decorating the clocks with crystals. She first applied crystals to her own Kit-Cats (around the eyes and on the ears and paws). But as word spread about her bejeweled timepieces and people asked where to buy them, Allied began making jeweled Kit-Cats for sale. These clocks were so popular between the late 1960s and early 1980s that Allied employed as many as 30 people at a time just to apply the jewels.

A Little Jolt

The early years had been good, but the 1980s weren't kind to Kit-Cat. As foreign companies bought up American clockmakers, manufacturing moved overseas, but Kit-Cat stayed in the United States. Business costs rose, and making the clocks' electrical motors became prohibitively expensive. That's where Woody Young came in. He bought the company in 1982 and experimented for years, trying to create a clock motor that could run on small batteries. It was slow going. In 1988, he needed a car battery to power Kit-Cat's motor, and even that could power the clock for only two days.

Then, in 1989, a breakthrough. With the help of his engineering team, Young managed to rework the clocks' motors so that they could run on two C batteries. Today that's all you need to keep Kit-Cat ticking for about six months at a time.

Kit-Cat Numbers:

- Original Kit-Cats (and today's classic design) were 15 $^1/_2$ inches tall and 4 inches wide; today, they sell for $39.99. The Kitty-Cat Klock is $^3/_4$ the size of the original and sells for $34.99.
- A Kit-Cat Klock's average life span is 25 years.
- Kit-Cats are movie stars! They've appeared in both *13 Going on 30* and the opening scene of *Back to the Future*.
- 128 Austrian crystals are used to decorate jeweled Klocks.

The Cat Bill Veto

Every once in a while, politicians
act wisely. Here is one such moment.

In 1949, the Illinois legislature passed a bill that would restrain the state's cats by requiring them to be escorted and on leashes when they went outside. The bill was the brainchild of a small group of bird lovers who wanted to protect what they believed was the state's vulnerable bird population. The bill came to rest on the desk of Governor Adlai Ewing Stevenson, and one swift flourish of the pen settled the matter: Veto!

Words of Wisdom

Here are the governor's witty remarks regarding his decision.

> I cannot agree that it should be the declared public policy of Illinois that a cat visiting a neighbor's yard or crossing the highways is a public nuisance. It is in the nature of cats to do a certain amount of unescorted roaming. Many live with their owners in apartments or other restricted premises, and I doubt if we want to make their every brief foray an opportunity for a small game hunt by zealous citizens—with traps or otherwise.

I am afraid this bill could only create discord, recrimination, and enmity. Also consider the owner's dilemma: To escort a cat abroad on a leash is against the nature of the cat, and to permit it to venture forth for exercise unattended into a night of new dangers is against the nature of the owner. Moreover, cats perform a useful service, particularly in rural areas, in combating rodents—work they necessarily perform alone and without regard for property lines.

We are all interested in protecting certain varieties of birds. That cats destroy some birds, I well know, but I believe this legislation would further but little the worthy cause to which its proponents give such unselfish effort. The problem of cat versus bird is as old as time. If we attempt to resolve it by legislation who knows but what we may be called upon to take sides as well in the age-old problems of dog versus cat, bird versus bird, or even bird versus worm. In my opinion, the State of Illinois and its local governing bodies already have enough to do without trying to control feline delinquency.

The (Bathroom) Door's Always Open

So, you want to say good-bye to plastic litter boxes, daily scooping, and an ammonia stink that makes your home smell like a biological weapons lab? Then say hello to the toilet-trained cat.

People make jokes all the time about toilet training their kitties: "Wouldn't it be great if my cat could use the toilet? And flush? Ah, the relief." Joking aside, some cats can actually be taught to use the toilet, though it takes time, a patient owner, and a kitty who's willing to be trained.

Training Essentials
1. A spayed or neutered litter-trained cat. The cat should be at least six months old and no older than 10 years.
2. A sturdy, shallow litter box, without a cover, that's no more than three or four inches deep so your cat can easily jump in and out of it.
3. Unscented, clumping cat litter.
4. Newspapers, a couple of sturdy cardboard boxes, or several old phone books.
5. A metal bowl that is the same diameter of your toilet.

Potty Training 101

Many animal behaviorists will tell you that teaching an old cat new toilet tricks is virtually impossible. And it's true—cats are a stubborn species and resistant to change. So don't be afraid to fail at potty training if your kitty just won't participate (if your cat hasn't responded to training after three months, she's probably not going to). But in reality, toilet training your cat doesn't involve teaching her anything too different from what she already does: she needs to relieve herself, and she does this while balancing herself and squatting on her hind legs. Getting her to do this on the toilet, instead of in the litter box, requires that you show her a new set of behaviors through a series of steps.

Step One:

Start by placing the litter box beside the toilet. When your cat gets used to this, you can raise the box a couple of inches each day by stacking newspapers, cardboard, or old phone books beneath it (raising the box helps your cat get used to jumping up to relieve herself). Just don't use magazines: they're too slippery and can cause the litter box and all its contents to spill onto the bathroom floor.

When the litter box reaches the height of the toilet seat, most cats will start jumping on the toilet seat in order to get into the litter box. Once this happens, you can move to the next step.

Step Two:

Place the metal bowl in the toilet seat; be sure the diameters of the bowl and the seat are compatible so the bowl doesn't fall in. Next, partially fill the bowl with litter. Remove the litter box from the bathroom, and your cat will (hopefully) start relieving herself in the litter-filled metal bowl. Once she does, slowly begin to reduce the amount of litter in the bowl.

Be sure to leave the bowl in the toilet all the time. If you remove it, kitty will get confused.

Step Three:

Next, teach your cat the proper squatting technique. You don't need to do this by example. All you have to do is manually place her four paws on the toilet seat until she can do it herself.

Step Four:

Finally, stop putting litter in the steel bowl, and fill it up with water instead. This way, your cat will get used to the plopping sounds that happen when she relieves herself.

Once she's learned how to perch on the toilet seat and has gotten used to relieving herself with her derriere hovering above water, you'll be able to remove the bowl.

And then—that's it! She's toilet trained.

41

You Know You're a
Cat Lover When . . .

- You get a pet fish or a bird to entertain your cats.
- You choose paper bags at the grocery store so your kitten will have something to play with.
- You feel lucky that your cat allows you to share her bed.
- You don't have health insurance, but your "baby" does.
- You don't take vacations because you can't bear to leave your cats home alone.
- You spend more on the cat's food than on your own.
- You bring in pictures of your "babies" to work and regale coworkers with stories of their milestones and accomplishments.
- You try to match your clothing to the color of your cat's fur.
- You intentionally spread out papers and warm laundry so the cats will have a place to sit.
- You make sure your cat drinks only bottled water.
- You leave your TV on the Animal Planet channel all day so your kitty won't get lonely while you're at work.
- You don't find any of these behaviors odd.

Nine Lives, Part 1

What would you do to save your cat?

How to Wreck a House in Four Hours

Two days after Tom and Ita Ryan-Casey of Thurles, Tipperary County, Ireland, discovered that one of their cats had gone missing, Ita heard purring from the yard and followed the sound to the house. Further examination revealed that the couple's six-month-old kitten, Richie, had gotten trapped in a gas vent pipe under one of the bedrooms. How Richie got there, no one knows, but she was stuck for four days until help arrived. A call to the local radio station and an on-air plea from the family motivated two local firms, an electronics security company and a drainage specialist firm, to help save the trapped kitten.

Using a camera and probe, rescuers identified Richie's exact location and then drilled a hole in the floor. A good effort, but the drill hit a water pipe, and the family had to bring in a plumber to keep the house from flooding. Finally, after four long hours of digging, the rescuers pulled the kitten free. The floors and pipes were destroyed (no word on what the total repairs cost), but Richie was safe and back in the eager arms of her family.

43

High-rising Feline

In March 2006, a cat named Piper bolted from her home in Summerville, South Carolina, and into the great suburban outdoors. When it was time to come in for the evening, Piper's family found her stuck some 80 feet up in a tree. Frantic calls to the fire department, animal control, even tree removal companies were to no avail; no one would help, and all assured the family that Piper would come down when she got hungry. But for eight long days, Piper stayed put, and the family waited and watched, trying (but not succeeding) to coax her out of the tree.

Local TV crews descended on Summerville to follow the story, and still the cat remained in the tree. Finally, help arrived, and as the rescuers began a tedious climb up the tree, Piper got scared. She moved onto a weak limb, the branch broke, and Piper plummeted to the ground. Fortunately, Piper fell spread-eagle, an instinctive feline response that allows cats to minimize the potential damage from a fall.

She landed on her feet and then bolted for the nearest cover—under a neighbor's car. Piper's vet diagnosed her with dehydration and muscle stiffness but assured everyone that she would make a full recovery. One life down; eight to go.

To read about more fantastic feline rescues, turn to page 178.

On the Strip, Part 2

*A couple more of the most popular cartoon
cats around. Part 1 appears on page 23.*

Garfield

Young Jim Davis was too sickly to work on his family's farm
in Indiana, so his mother kept him supplied with pencils
and paper and encouraged him to draw. When he graduated from college, he got a job as assistant to Tom Ryan,
creator of the syndicated comic strip *Tumbleweeds*. A few
years later, Davis went to New York to sell his own strip—
Gnorm Gnat, about an insect. Everyone turned it down.
"They told me nobody could identify with a bug," Davis
says. So he looked for a subject people could identify with
and noticed there were lots of dogs in successful comic
strips—Snoopy, Marmaduke, Belvedere—but few cats.

So he decided to fashion a cat character after his "big,
opinionated, stubborn" grandfather, James Garfield Davis,
and sold it to United Features, a newspaper and syndication company. The strip, called *Garfield*, debuted in 41
newspapers on June 19, 1978.

During the 1980s, *Garfield* moved beyond comic strips.
Merchandising for the cartoon became a billion-dollar-
a-year industry: between 1987 and 1989, 225 million
suction-cupped Garfield dolls sold. The cat also became a

star of the big and small screens. Between 1982 and 1995, 13 Garfield television series and specials aired, and the orange kitty has appeared in two feature films.

Hobbes

Calvin and Hobbes creator Bill Watterson started cartooning when his dreams of becoming an astronaut dissolved. The youngster's lack of aptitude in math and science kept him from pursuing a career in space. But his wit and skill with a pen provided a very different career path.

Watterson was born in 1958 in Washington, D.C., where his parents were involved in politics. As a child, he was a fan of *Peanuts*, *Pogo*, and *Krazy Kat* cartoons and, in the early 1980s, he took a job drawing political cartoons for the *Cincinnati Post*. He was fired after only two weeks, the result of a professional falling out with the newspaper's editor, and then spent four years drawing advertisements for local grocery stores.

During that time, he also pitched ideas to comic syndicates. Six-year-old Calvin (originally called Marvin) and his stuffed tiger, Hobbes, were secondary characters in one of Watterson's pitches. He ultimately turned them into the stars of their own strip, and in 1985, Universal Press Syndicate decided to run the comic.

Calvin and Hobbes ran from November 18, 1985, to December 31, 1995. This strip about the adventures of a boy and his imaginary (or is he?) best pal—a stuffed tiger—became one of the most popular comic strips in the world. In 1985, *Calvin and Hobbes* ran in about 35 papers. Ten years later, it was printed in more than 2,400 newspapers worldwide.

Watterson quit drawing the comic for newspapers in 1995 and throughout his career has refused to license *Calvin and Hobbes* for merchandise, movies, or TV. But fans can still find the mischievous duo in one of several book collections. More than 30 million copies have sold so far. And in 2005, Watterson and Andrews McMeel Publishing released a complete collection of Calvin and Hobbes cartoons. The three-volume, hardbound, 1,440-page edition, weighs 23 pounds and includes, among other things, every printed *Calvin and Hobbes* comic—some that never made it into the newspapers—and an introduction from Watterson himself.

* * *

Did You Know?

Calvin and Hobbes has been translated into dozens of foreign languages, including Portuguese, Russian, and Korean. And depending on the country, Calvin and Hobbes may go by different names. In Brazil, they are Calvin and Haroldo; in Finland, Lassi and Leevi; and in Taiwan, Caihwon and Hohaw.

Cats in Song

Match these cat-titled ditties to their singer or band.

1. "What's New Pussycat"   A. Stray Cats

2. "Stray Cat Strut"   B. Harry Chapin

3. "My Grandmother's Cat"   C. Phoebe Buffay

4. "Everybody Wants to Be a Cat"   D. Tom Jones

5. "Black Cat"   E. Peggy Lee

6. "Cat Fever"   F. The Cat Pack

7. "Cat's in the Cradle"   G. Janet Jackson

8. "Smelly Cat"   H. Little Feat

9. "The Siamese Cat Song"   I. Garrison Keillor

For answers, turn to page 220.

The Kitten Rules

Cat lovers know that every household should have a benevolent dictator. That's where a new kitten comes in. Here are five things you might be surprised to learn your kitten needs.

1. A baby-proofed room

Kittens are new to the independent world, and they need a warm, private space where they can hide when life gets overwhelming. They do best in rooms cleared of dangers such as electrical cords, temperamental tomcats, reactionary dogs, and curious toddlers. The "room" doesn't actually have to be an entire room, however. A closet will do. Bathtubs are also good, although morning showers become problematic.

2. A warm napping spot

Old towels, blankets, and sweaters make cozy nap spots. Added comfort may also come from a hot water bottle tucked under the bedding or a ticking clock to simulate the heartbeat of the kitten's mother.

3. Toys, glorious toys!

Small balls, bells, toy mice, and a variety of objects the kitten can toss about or pounce on make great playthings. Humans may think the kitten is just being cute when he plays with his toys, but in fact, he's developing the motor skills of a predator and learning to be the defender of his domain.

4. Space for a good scratch*

Any new kitten needs a first scratching post; scratching keeps your cat in shape by working the muscles in her front paws and chest. Usually, the first scratching post is an owner's bare hand or arm. But soon, kitty needs something less animate. Most cats prefer scratching posts covered with carpet or sisal.

Note: Failure to comply with #4 may result in ripped pantyhose and torn couch cushions.

5. Daily spa treatments

This service should include grooming with a brush to maintain a soft, sleek, tangle-free coat. Metal bristles can scratch kitty's delicate skin, however, so a brush with soft plastic or rubber bristles is best.

* * *

"There is no more intrepid explorer than a kitten."
—*Jules Champfleury, French novelist*

Persians and Siamese

If it's a high-class cat you want, look to the East.

One Fancy Pedigree

Modern Persians trace their ancestry to long-haired cats imported to Europe from Turkey and Central Asia. The breed's exact lineage is unknown. But historians' best guess is that Turkish Angoras, found in Europe since the Renaissance, bred with other long-haired cats from Persia (now Iran), India, and Afghanistan beginning in the 17th century; these pairings probably produced today's breed.

Whatever their origin, Persians, with their baby faces and powder-puff bodies, rapidly became status symbols among wealthy Europeans. Many 18th- and 19th-century European portraits depict society ladies holding Persian cats. And these felines never lost their popularity—more than 60 percent of the cats registered with the Cat Fanciers' Association today are Persians. But they're expensive. Most purebred kittens start at about $500, and they can cost more than $2,000 apiece.

The Persians' status extends to their upkeep as well. These are high-maintenance cats. Their fur is too long for self-grooming—some show cats have tail fur that's eight inches long! So owners have to comb and brush their

Persians regularly to prevent tangles and mats. But devotees don't mind—Persians are affectionate and playful, and they make wonderful pets.

Bangkok or Bust

Rivaling Persians for the top rung of the elite-breed ladder is the Siamese. These cats have been around for centuries and hail from Siam (now Thailand). According to ancient Thai law, only the king and other royals were allowed to own Siamese cats. And when a royal died, his Siamese cat went to live at a nearby temple, pampered and fawned over by the monks and priests. Siamese cats living in these temples slept on satin pillows and ate whatever and whenever they wanted, because the Southeast Asians believed the felines sheltered and protected the souls of their deceased former owners.

During the late 19th century, Siamese cats sailed on merchant ships from Bangkok to London, and soon after, they made their way to the United States. In 1878, David B. Sickels, the U.S. consul in Bangkok, sent a female Siamese cat to the wife of President Rutherford B. Hayes. "I am informed that it is the first attempt ever made to send a Siamese cat to America," the diplomat wrote. Lucy Hayes named the cat Siam, and her arrival ignited interest in the breed in the United States. By 1900, Siamese cats were appearing in American cat shows.

We Are Siamese if You Please

These royal cats of Siam look as elegant as their history suggests they are. They're thin, sleek, and come in a number of color combinations: light or dark brown, gray, cream, even tortoiseshell patterns. But the telltale sign of a Siamese is its light-colored body and points (darker coloring on the cat's ears, face, paws, and tail). This coloration pattern is the work of a genetic trait that restricts color to the cooler parts of a Siamese's body.

* * *

Feline Fact

Siamese cats have served as the foundation for a number of new breeds, including the Balinese (a long-haired Siamese), the Tonkinese (a Siamese-Burmese mix), the Havana Brown (a cross between a Siamese and a black domestic shorthair), and the Ocicat (a Siamese and Abyssinian mix).

* * *

Cats are more likely to respond to names that are one to two syllables long and that end in y or ie.

Hemingway's Key West Cats

Novelist Ernest Hemingway loved women, drinking, and cats—probably in that order. But if legend holds true, no ordinary feline would do for this storyteller: he preferred the six-toed variety.

The Six-Toed Darlings

During the late 1920s and 1930s, Hemingway lived in Key West, Florida, with his second wife, Pauline. There, he had a reputation around town for being a carouser who frequented neighborhood bars, but he also loved cats. At some point (when is up for debate), Hemingway came into possession of a white, six-toed cat he named Snowball. He doted on the cat, and some historians claim that when Hemingway traveled, he wrote letters to Pauline asking about Snowball, who lived and flourished under his master's watchful eye.

A Cat's Life

The Key West home where Hemingway once lived is now the Hemingway House and Museum. It houses many relics from the writer's life and as many as 60 cats, about half of whom are polydactyl (with multiple toes). Some of the cats have as many as eight toes, and according to the museum, all are descendants of Snowball.

These felines are treated like royalty at the museum. Curators tend to their every need. Bowls of food sit beneath most of the grounds' palm trees, and there are always hands willing to give a stroke or scratch. The cats also freely roam among the gardens and come and go as they please inside the house.

The Truth Shall Set You Flea

The details surrounding the cats' pedigree depend on whom you ask, however. Hemingway House docents insist that the writer received his first six-toed cat while he was still living in Key West. But Hemingway's son Patrick takes issue with this story and maintains that his father received Snowball en route to Cuba—after he had divorced Pauline and left Key West for good. In fact, Patrick claims that Hemingway never had cats in Key West at all. Although his father loved cats, Patrick says, Pauline preferred peacocks, and the polydactyl cats didn't appear in his father's life until later, when the birds were no longer around.

Although Patrick's story doesn't explain how all the multi-toed cats ended up in Florida, he neither disputes the claim that the six-toed cats are Snowball's descendants nor offers an explanation for how the current brood of cats ended up making the Hemingways' Key West house their home. But sometimes a good story is more important than distinguishing fact from fiction. Hemingway himself certainly appreciated a well-told tale.

* * *

Watering Hole

Because there are so many cats living at the Hemingway House, they need a pretty big water bowl, and Ernest Hemingway himself left a relic in the backyard that the museum uses for just this purpose. The makeshift vessel is a converted urinal from Sloppy Joe's, a Key West bar that was one of the writer's favorite haunts. Hemingway salvaged the urinal when the owner was ready to throw it out—Hemingway told the bar owner he'd spent so much time using it that he might as well keep it. Not surprisingly, Pauline didn't much like the looks of a urinal in her backyard and had it tiled to make it look a little less . . . functional. Today, it's a water fountain where the museum cats gather to drink, swap meows, and trade tall tales.

The Real Cat Herders

In the world of information technology, any impossibly complicated technological feat is called "herding cats"; one company turned that phrase into a memorable commercial.

A cowboy sits by the fire rolling a ball of yarn. A group of cats circles a helpless rancher who tries to direct them. A fluffy Persian runs in slow motion, bathed in the golden light of a setting sun. A weathered cowboy cleans cat hair off his duster with a lint-roller. It was only 60 seconds long, but the cat-herding commercial that aired during the third quarter of Superbowl XXXIV was, for many viewers, better than the game itself.

Creative types at the Minneapolis-based Fallon McElligott ad agency came up with the commercial. The agency created the television spot for an information technology company called EDS (Electronic Data Systems), founded in the 1960s by Ross Perot. EDS hoped the clever commercial would help woo new talent.

How'd They Do That?
The cat-herding commercial used real cats and real cowboys to spoof a cattle-type roundup of cats being driven into town. The spot was filmed at the Tejon Ranch, 70 miles north of Los Angeles, and much of the dialogue was

improvised. The cowboys talked about herding and ranching but substituted "cats" for "cattle."

The cat herd was actually made up of only 60 cats. Special effects multiplied that number to thousands. And as for how the directors got the kitties to ford a river, one ad exec said only, "Catnip in the water."

We Are the Cat Herders

The ad debuted on January 30, 2000, during the Super Bowl. The company's Web site got 2 million hits the next day, 10 times its normal site traffic. Newspapers across the country ran articles about the ad. The *Fort Worth Star Telegram* said, "EDS's kitty trail-drive commercial is hysterical. Ross Perot should have had these guys do his campaign ads." Even President Bill Clinton mentioned the commercial in a speech, saying, "That's the best ad I saw on television last year." Clients bombarded EDS with business opportunities, and employees proudly began to call themselves the "cat herders."

The commercial ran only a few times, and several years have passed since its Super Bowl debut. But EDS continues to receive e-mail about it. The company initially included an interactive cat-herding game on its Web site, as well as a making-of video. Those are now long gone as EDS has gone back to its actual business— solving information and technology problems. But the cat-herding commercial still lives on the Internet, just a Google search away.

* * *

Jack and the Bear

In June 2006, an orange-and-white tabby named Jack encountered a black bear in his suburban New Jersey neighborhood. Unwilling to relinquish his territory, Jack chased the bear up a tree and stood guard on the ground, hissing and snarling for 15 minutes before the bear ran away. Jack gave chase and the bear scurried up another tree. Jack's owner finally noticed the brouhaha and called Jack inside (she also called animal control about the bear), but she needn't have feared. Jack, it seemed, had everything under control.

The Cat's a Good Sign

*For Depression-era hoboes, a cat sketched
on a fence post or window meant good luck.*

During the early 20th century and through the Great
Depression, millions of Americans were out of work.
Some of those (mostly single men, but also women and
children) became hoboes, migrants who traveled from
town to town looking for work, free meals, and a place to
sleep. A culture evolved among these travelers, one that
frightened some in the mainstream. Many parents warned
their children to stay away from "hobo jungles," parts of
town (usually deserted areas near railroad tracks) where
hoboes congregated to talk, share stories, or hop onto
freight trains headed for other areas. Even charitable families often refused to allow hoboes into their homes, instead
giving the transients meals outside on the porch and offering them barns to sleep in.

The Writing on the Wall

For the hoboes, though, theirs was an
intricate culture. They had rules:
their creed was "A hobo is a man who
travels and is willing to work," an

effort to distinguish hoboes from bums who just wanted handouts. They even had their own written language, symbols that one hobo drew in an out-of-the-way spot— scratched into a fence post, perhaps, or drawn in the dust on a dirty basement window—to pass along a little bit of information about the inhabitants of a particular home. A series of five circles, for example, meant that the family was likely to give money to workers passing through. The number 18 translated to "I ate" (I-8), declaring that the previous hobo had been given a meal. Other symbols warned of police and dogs. But one symbol—a sketch of a cat—meant that at least one benevolent and kindhearted woman lived in the home. So when a hobo came upon a new town, he looked for the cat symbol to identify the homes that would be welcoming and might provide him with a hot meal and a warm place to sleep.

* * *

Charles I ruled England from 1625 to 1649. According to legend, he had a lucky black cat, and as civil war gripped the country, Charles became convinced that his cat would keep him safe. He even assigned guards to protect the feline. It didn't work. The cat was killed, and one day later, Charles was arrested and eventually sentenced to death by beheading.

La Dolce Vita

In Rome, wild cats live the sweet life.

Cat Ladies Say, "*Mangia!*"

An estimated 200,000 to 300,000 wild cats live in Rome and are free to wander the Eternal City. More than 200 cats make their home in the Colosseum area alone. And even though the cats are feral—born wild or abandoned— they live pretty well, thanks to the *gattare*, or cat ladies, who feed the animals table scraps of spaghetti or canned cat food.

Anyone might be a cat lady: from society matrons to bag ladies to schoolgirls. Even men can be cat ladies— although the majority of *gattare* are older women. The most famous *gattara* was 1940s and 1950s Italian film star Anna Magnani (whose most famous role was as Pina in Roberto Rossellini's *Open City*). During breaks from work and until her death in the 1970s, Magnani regularly fed cats near the Teatro Argentina opera house.

But it isn't just the *gattare* who cater to the city's home-less cats. Even restaurant owners get in on the act. They leave heaping plates of pasta for the cats and sometimes put out linen-covered tables in Rome's alleys so the felines can feast in style.

A Sanctuary to Call Their Own

There is also a cat sanctuary located at the Torre Argentina, the temple where Brutus stabbed his rival Julius Caesar. The site was excavated in 1929, and soon after, it became a favorite hangout for the local tabbies. Because the cats were there, the *gattare* came. And in 1994, some of them organized a nonprofit agency, the Torre Argentina Cat Sanctuary, to shelter and care for needy and abandoned cats. Today, many of the cats live beneath the ruins in comfortable cages that line the earthen walls. Each cage is tagged with the cat resident's name, medical history, and feeding schedule.

To fund the endeavor, Torre Argentina solicits funds by setting up displays of caged cats around Rome's major tourist attractions. Volunteers decorate the displays with balloons and signs that explain their mission, and they set out donation cans. Torre Argentina also maintains an adoption Web site, with photos of the cats to entice prospective adoptive parents. If you don't live in Italy but still want to help one of these cats, Torre Argentina offers a sponsorship program. For $15 a month, you can provide food and medical care for

the cat of your choice, and you'll receive a photo and regular updates about your sponsored pet.

Scratch Behind Their Ears: It's the Law

With the *gattare* and the folks at Torre Argentina around,
one might think Roman cats don't need any more help.
But the government has gotten involved too. An Italian
law passed in the mid-1990s guarantees that strays have
the right to stay wherever they are born. So if you live in
Rome and wake up one morning to a litter of kittens on
your doorstep, you'd better get used to them: they are
yours for life.

This law also requires citizens to make sure that any
stray cats who adopt Roman households are fed and given
medical help when they need it. It is illegal to put down
these wild cats—unless they have incurable diseases or are
suffering. But they can be neutered or spayed, and the
local government provides this service for free, as well as
regular checkups afterward.

Rats! Where Did Those Cats Come From?

The first cats came to Rome aboard trading ships from
Egypt. For many years, Romans reaped the benefits of
having a hefty feline population, especially in the 1300s,
when the bubonic plague first arrived in Italy. Infected
fleas on rats spread the plague, though no one knew that
then. They only knew the rats had something to do with
it, and since cats helped keep the rat population down,

Rome's cats helped to protect the city from that disease.

But not everyone appreciated the cats. During the 14th and 15th centuries, the Roman Catholic Church considered cats to be associates of witches, and some church members hunted and killed the animals. After the feline population was thinned out, the rodent population exploded—and so did the number of plague fatalities. As more people died from the disease, clergy and laymen alike realized that a larger cat population would help keep the city healthy, so they eased up on the cats for a while. Once the plague was under control, though, church representatives started killing the cats again. This continued for

more than three centuries, until witch trials lost support in Europe during the 1700s.

These days, the cats in Rome don't do much to keep the rat population down. The city's rodents feast on discarded food scraps and are often as big as the cats themselves. But with cat ladies around to bring them bowls of food, Roman cats no longer need to hunt.

Cat Capers, Part 1

*Andy Warhol once said that everyone would eventually have
15 minutes of fame. We aren't sure if this prediction applied to
felines too, but these cats certainly have spent time in the spotlight.*

Headline: *Lost Cat Logs 30,000 Miles, but Denied
Frequent-Flyer Miles*
The Feline Star: Tabitha
What Happened: In June 1994, aspiring actress Carol
Ann Timmel, 26, of Westchester County, New York,
checked two of her cats as baggage for a Tower Air flight
from New York to Los Angeles. But when she got off the
plane in Los Angeles, there was only one cat left in the
cage. The other one, a three-year-old named Tabitha, had
escaped into the bowels of the plane during the flight.

Tower Air refused to ground the plane long enough for
a thorough search. Instead, the airline kept the plane in
operation and had ground crews search the cargo hold at
every stop. The plane logged more than 30,000 miles traveling to New York, Los Angeles, Miami, and Puerto Rico,
while Timmel sued to take the plane out of commission.
Twelve days later she prevailed. The plane was grounded
in New York for 24 hours while more than 100 Tower
employees—and one psychic—scoured the plane looking
for the cat. Timmel herself found the cat after she called

out to Tabitha and the kitty returned her calls. "The cat didn't look out of whack," one Tower employee told reporters. "It just looked like it needed a good dinner."

Aftermath: Timmel sold Tabitha's life story to a TV producer for $30,000 . . . but her own acting career never took off. At last report, she was working in a Los Angeles gardening store.

Headline: *Give This Cat Some Credit—but Not That Much Credit*

The Feline Star: Theo Theoklitos

What Happened: In October 1992, Theo's owner, Helen Krikris, sent in an application for a rebate on cat food. Somehow Theo, a six-year-old black cat, ended up on a bunch of mailing lists and since then, he's received as much mail as his owner, including video club offers, credit card applications, and discount magazine subscriptions. (One flyer read, "So you think you're smarter than your cat?") He's even become a finalist in Ed McMahon's $10 million sweepstakes.

Aftermath: Newspapers all over the country picked up the tale of junk mail gone crazy. Meanwhile, Krikris decided she knew why Theo's so popular. "You know," she says, "these people who send him all this mail probably think he's a wealthy Greek shipping magnate because of his name."

To read about more cat capers,
turn to page 112.

*   *   *

Cat's Best Friend

The Wildlife Images Rehabilitation and Education Center in Oregon has been saving animals since 1981. Two of its most famous residents were best pals Cat (an orange tabby) and Griz (a 600-pound grizzly bear).

Cat and Griz met in 1995 and bonded over lunch. One afternoon, as Griz ripped into a meal in his enclosure at Wildlife Images, Cat approached slowly. He was just a stray kitten then, abandoned and hoping for something to eat. For a moment, the animals just stared at one another, but then Griz pulled a bit of meat off of his plate and offered it to the kitty. Cat grabbed it with his teeth and escaped to safety under a bush. Soon, the pair became inseparable. Keepers at the animal sanctuary had trouble catching Cat; he was afraid of them. But he was completely unfazed by Griz. At night, Cat slept curled up under the grizzly's chin. And during the day, he hid in the brush and swatted his pal as the bear ambled by.

Proverbial Pussycats

Felines appear in proverbs from many different countries. Here are some of our favorites.

The cat's a saint when there are no mice about.

—*Japan*

A house without either a cat or a dog is the house of a scoundrel.

—*Portugal*

Handsome cats and fat dung heaps are the signs of a good farmer.

—*France*

Happy is the home with at least one cat.

—*Italy*

If stretching were wealth, the cat would be rich.

—*Africa*

The cat who frightens mice away is as good as the cat who eats them.

—*Germany*

Beware people who dislike cats.

—*Ireland*

Pint-sized Pollocks

Monet. Manet. Picasso . . . Frank?

A new artistic movement is afoot. The painters create abstract art, and viewers can't get enough of the artists' innovative uses of color, their mastery of technique. But it's not just the work that sets these painters apart. It's also that they are cats.

Painting Pusses

There's Oscar, an orange tabby from Saskatchewan, Canada. Owner Anna Scott recognized his potential when Oscar started playing with the water in his dish. He swirled it around with his paw before drinking it, and Scott thought he might be trying to express himself. So she mixed food coloring and water, laid down some paper, and let Oscar go to town. The result was a collection of blue, green, and red abstract watercolors that Scott, an artist herself, showed at a local gallery.

Other cat painters, like Kali and Figaro from Chicago, use nontoxic paint to create swirling red, yellow, and blue patterns.

And Frank, once an orphaned feline artist living at an animal shelter in Oregon, used suede for his canvas and crafted a piece called *Three Blind Mice* that made it into a local art show. Patrons sipped wine and called Frank "Pollock with paws," an allusion to what they believed were similarities between the two artists' styles. All this attention not only got Frank's paintings into the public eye; it also got him a home. The cat was adopted just before the show's opening night by a family who enjoyed his work.

Everything's for Sale

The kitties' paintings don't just adorn the refrigerators and office walls of their owners. These paintings go on sale at art galleries, animal shelters, and regional shows all over the United States. The San Francisco SPCA, for example, sells cat art prints for $15 apiece. And a cat named Bud D. Holly, who lives in California, commands up to $250 for an original painting.

Seeing Is Believing

Cat painters are slowly integrating into the art world. OK, yes, they're taking it one paw print at a time. But they're making a name for themselves.

A 1994 book called *Why Cats Paint* prompted much of the recent activity. The lighthearted book shows several cat painters at work and gave people like Anna Scott the idea that her kitty should put paw to paper. But science and history seem to back up the cat-as-painter theory as well.

Most cat owners know that kitties mark their territories, often by smearing their waste in a swirly pattern. This releases scents to warn other cats that the area has been claimed. Some biologists believe that cat painters are doing something similar, especially in the cases of felines who use paints that contain ammonia.

Ancient cultures also recognized cats' artistic abilities. The Egyptians worshipped cats, and in the 1980s, archeologists uncovered the tomb of the ancient ruler Aperia that contained not only mummified feline remains, but paw-painted funerary scrolls.

*   *   *

"Cats always seem so very wise
when staring with their half-closed eyes.
Can they be thinking, 'I'll be nice, and
maybe she will feed me twice'"?
—*Bette Midler*

Britain's Chief Mouser

*Here's how a stray cat became the subject of
national inquiry and official questioning
in the House of Commons.*

Enter Humphrey

In October 1989, a black-and-white one-year-old stray cat
wandered into No. 10 Downing Street, the British prime
minister's official residence. Margaret Thatcher was in
office at the time, and Britain needed an official cat: the
country's previous "feline minister" (Wilberforce) had died
the year before. Named Humphrey (after Sir Humphrey
Appleby in the TV series *Yes, Minister*), the new kitty
remained at Downing Street even after Thatcher left
office. In all, Humphrey lived with three prime minis-
ters—Thatcher, John Major, and Tony Blair—and took on
an official title: Chief Mouser to the Cabinet Office. The
national budget even included money for his keep: 100
pounds a year.

A cat at Downing Street isn't unusual. For more than
two centuries, the prime minister of England has kept a
cat. But this particular feline got a little more press than
the rest. During his eight years in residence, Humphrey
was accused of attacking a nest of robins (though John
Major furiously defended his honor), was nearly run over

by the tires of Bill Clinton's Cadillac, and was presumed dead for three months in 1995 before he was found alive and well, hanging out at the Royal Army Medical College. On his return to No. 10, Humphrey issued an official statement: "I have had a wonderful holiday at the Royal Army Medical College, but it is nice to be back and I am looking forward to the new parliamentary session."

Enter Tony Blair

In May 1997, Tony Blair became prime minister of Great Britain and moved his family into No. 10 Downing Street. Rumors that Mrs. Blair was allergic to cats and that the Blairs weren't cat people led many Britons to worry about Humphrey's fate. But the family issued a formal statement that Humphrey would continue to be welcome at Downing Street; No. 10 was his home and would remain so. Humphrey and Mrs. Blair even took a picture together to prove there was no animosity between cat and mistress. But six months later, in November 1997, Humphrey's vet diagnosed him with a kidney condition. At first, an official memo circulated among government officials, informing them of Humphrey's condition, explaining his new diet, and imploring them not to feed him any treats. But soon after, the Downing Street cat moved to an undisclosed countryside location with a Cabinet Office worker so that he could retire from public life and live out his days in a less stressful environment.

Enter Politics

Critics of Tony Blair's politics immediately accused the prime minister of deceiving the public and euthanizing the cat instead of retiring him as reported. One Tory Member of Parliament demanded proof that the cat was still alive, and journalists reminded the public of Mrs. Blair's alleged allergies. Eventually, the accusations became more than the Blair administration could ignore.

To appease the press, public, and politicians, Downing Street officials took members of the media to Humphrey's new country home and allowed him to be photographed for the papers. But even that wasn't enough. Some journalists and photographers expressed suspicion over the seemingly good health of the presumably ailing cat.

The Humphrey hubbub eventually fizzled, but it never died down completely. In March 2005, a British newspaper, the *Daily Telegraph*, asked the government for information about the cat, citing the Freedom of Information Act as part of its demand. Later that year, another paper, the *Independent*, reported that Humphrey was "alive and well."

Then, in April 2006, came the official announcement Britons had been dreading: Humphrey, No. 10's Chief Mouser, had died of kidney failure. He was 17 years old, not bad for a stray who wandered into No. 10 Downing Street and charmed an entire country.

* * *

The Lion Man

The world's oldest statue is of a cat. The Lion Man statue, a 32,000-year-old, one-foot-tall piece carved from mammoth ivory, was found in a cave in Southern Germany. Archeologists aren't sure what the Old Stone Age culture used the lion statue for, but they speculate that it was a religious or magical relic. Since lions at that time were far superior to human hunters, scientists theorize that the ancients carved the Lion Man and others like it (a second, smaller but similar, statue was found nearby) in the hopes of channeling some of the lions' hunting skills.

* * *

A cat is a lion in a jungle of small bushes.
—Indian proverb

A Wild Kingdom

*Off a dusty Arizona highway just 45 minutes from Las Vegas,
Nevada, live Jonathan Kraft and his collection of really cool cats.*

A tiger skulks about. A lion roars in the distance. A
serval's yellow eyes keep a close watch for intruders.
You might think you've stepped into an African wildlife
scene, but really, you're just visiting an animal sanctuary
in Valentine, Arizona. Called Keepers of the Wild, the
sanctuary has been around since the mid-1990s and is the
pet project of Jonathan Kraft, a former Las Vegas per-
former who once ran an exotic animal theme park on the
Strip. It's a life he's not proud of now—"I started out buy-
ing two baby tigers for all the wrong reasons," he admits—
but it did provide him with a unique perspective on the
plight of exotic animals (especially big cats kept as pets) in
America.

Where the Wild Things Are

According to Kraft, there are about 15,000 wild cats kept
as pets in the United States. And no matter how cute and
cuddly the animals are as babies, they're still predators
who grow up to be more than their owners can handle.
When that happens, the animals are often abandoned,

abused, or euthanized. Kraft tries to step in before it gets to that point.

Many of the animals who live at the sanctuary have been donated by owners who just can't take care of them. An African serval named Jordan, for example, came to the sanctuary in 2003 after her owners decided she was too dangerous to handle. A Bengal tiger named Zeus came to Kraft by way of a Minnesota couple who kept him as a pet until state animal control officials found out (tigers are illegal as house pets in Minnesota). Kraft stepped in and took the tiger before he could be euthanized. And then there's Curtis, a cougar who once belonged to Guns N' Roses guitarist, Slash. Curtis roamed Slash's house freely, a practice that led to run-ins with visiting humans. When Curtis finally bit someone, Slash donated him to Kraft's sanctuary.

Some of the animals require more extensive intervention, and Kraft has built a reputation as a man who will stop at nothing to save an injured or abused wild cat. The patient of whom he's most proud is a lion named Sabu. Sabu belonged to a Las Vegas woman who kept him in a small cage in her yard. When Kraft found him in the mid-1990s, Sabu weighed only 100 pounds (healthy lions weigh 200 to 250 pounds); he suffered from rickets, arthritis, severe malnutrition, and a broken jaw. And as a result of a botched declawing procedure, he had deformed feet that made it painful for him to walk. Kraft rescued the animal from his horrific surroundings and took him back to the sanctuary, where a veterinarian told him that the most humane course of action was to euthanize the lion. Kraft refused and instead nursed Sabu back to health himself. He got vitamins and antibiotics from the vet, hand-fed the lion, and slept with him in a room whose floor was covered with thick carpeting and straw to protect the animal's delicate feet.

Weeks went by, and Sabu slowly regained his strength. After a year at Kraft's sanctuary, the lion was running, jumping, and playing. He was also enamored with the man who had saved his life. One volunteer said that on seeing Kraft, Sabu would wrap his front paws around the handler, "clasping [Kraft] to his chest as though they hadn't seen each other for years." Sabu lived at the sanctuary for six and a half years before he died of natural causes in 2001.

Call of the Wild

Today, more than 30 wild cats live at Kraft's Arizona sanctuary. These include bobcats, tigers, lions, leopards, and others. There are also several non-feline species, including monkeys, wolves, birds, iguanas, and turtles. All these animals need lots of room to roam, so Kraft built a new 175-acre nature park in 2006.

The animals and their new habitat are funded by private donations and through tours of the sanctuary given by Kraft and his volunteers. People who stop by should be forewarned that the habitats are constructed from the animals' point of view, not the visitors', so Kraft can't guarantee that tourists will see a lion or a tiger every time. But that hasn't stopped the visitors from coming. Each year, about 250,000 guests stop by the Keepers of the Wild sanctuary, hoping to catch a glimpse of the exotic animals and of the man who has dedicated his life to giving them all a safe and happy home.

The Rescuers

Keepers of the Wild is one of several big cat sanctuaries in the United States. Here are four more:

Big Cat Rescue: *Tampa, Florida*
- Rescuers of lions, tigers, jaguars, ocelots, and others
- Open for public tours

EARS (The Endangered Animal Rescue Sanctuary): *Citra, Florida*
- Rescuers of cougars, lions, and tigers
- EARS isn't zoned as a public facility, so the sanctuary isn't open to the public for tours. But volunteers do schedule visits for sponsors who buy memberships to the facility (the memberships help fund the organization).

Tiger Creek Wildlife Rescue: *Tyler, Texas*
- Rescuers of tigers, leopards, cougars, and lions
- Open for public tours

Animal Ark: *Reno, Nevada*
- Rescuers of cheetahs, tigers, bobcats, lynx, and cougars
- Open for public tours

Jokes on Us, Part 2

Some more fantastic feline humor.
(Part 1 appears on page 12.)

Where did the kittens go to see art?
A mew-seum

What makes a cat dizzy?
Giving him a tailspin

Why was the kitty late for the party?
Her fur coat was at the cleaners.

What color do cats like
best?
Purr-ple

How do cats mail
letters?
Using fur-class mail

The Biggest 'Fraidy
Cat in Hollywood

*Although technically the king of the forest, Oz's
Cowardly Lion is anything but lionhearted.*

The Cowardly Lion gained worldwide fame in 1939
when MGM's *The Wizard of Oz* hit the big screen.
But by then, he'd been around for almost four decades as a
star of literature, stage, and the silent screen. And his role
in popular culture continues today.

The Book
In 1900, author L. Frank Baum published *The Wonderful
Wizard of Oz*, the story of Dorothy Gale and her adven-
tures in a mysterious land called Oz. During her foray into
Oz, Dorothy meets many quirky, charming, and sometimes
scary characters, including the Cowardly Lion.

Thirteen more Baum-penned Oz books followed the
original, and the Cowardly Lion accompanies Dorothy
on many of the adventures in those stories. In 1929, he
even appeared in his own book entitled *The Cowardly
Lion of Oz*, written by Ruth Plumly Thompson, who carried on the series and wrote 19 Oz works after Baum's
death.

His First Trip to Broadway

The Cowardly Lion first hit the stage in 1902. Baum, composer Paul Tietjens, and director Julian Mitchell brought *The Wizard of Oz* (they dropped the word *wonderful* for this first stage production, and the title has gone without it in most productions since) to Broadway. The show was a hit and ran from 1902 to 1911.

Silent Films

There were at least two silent films made from Baum's first book: one in 1910 and one in 1925. The lion appears in both, though he's not as dynamic or as prominent a character as he is in the 1939 film. Few people saw these movies, and the 1925 version didn't even make it to most of the theaters that ordered it. Chadwick Pictures, the company that made the film, went bankrupt during production and wasn't able to distribute the movie as promised.

The 1939 Hit

By far, the Cowardly Lion with whom most people are familiar is the one who appears in the 1939 MGM movie. In that version the lion (played by Bert Lahr) is a golden-haired feline with a booming voice. Trivia abounds about his character and the making of that movie; here are a few bits:

- Lahr's costume weighed 90 pounds and was made from two real lion skins.

- His makeup was so elaborate and heavy that he couldn't eat without ruining it. For weeks, Lahr subsisted on milk shakes and soup but finally decided he'd had enough. So he ate his regular lunch every day and then had his makeup redone for shooting.
- Technicians on a walkway above the soundstages worked like puppeteers to manipulate the lion's tail.

Back to Broadway

In 1974, the Cowardly Lion (played by actor Ted Ross) returned to Broadway in *The Wiz*. This play (also a 1978 film starring Diana Ross and Michael Jackson) was an urbanized retelling of *The Wizard of Oz* story. It featured an all–African American cast and Dorothy as an inner-city girl who gets whisked away from her New York City neighborhood to the magical world of Oz. The play ran until January 28, 1979, and was revived for two weeks in 1984.

More recently, the Cowardly Lion appears in the Broadway musical *Wicked*. This play, based on a novel by Gregory Maguire, premiered in 2003 and tells the story of the Wicked Witch of the West's rise to wickedness and power. The Cowardly Lion has a minor role as an animal rescued by the young witch; he grows up cowardly because he was never forced to fend for himself in the wild. *Wicked* continues to enjoy success on Broadway, in London, and on tour throughout the United States.

Easy Rider

Cuddle Bug goes where few cats have gone before.

Back in March 2005, as Torri Hutchinson cruised along Highway 15 in Idaho, she noticed a man trying to flag her down. He was gesturing frantically and shouting to her. Hutchinson wasn't sure why he wanted her attention or what he was trying to communicate. Plus, all of his enthusiasm made her a little nervous. She did wonder, though, if the ski rack atop her car might be coming loose, so she pulled over. The man stopped behind her, and to be safe, Hutchinson kept her car running and her doors locked. The man, however, jumped out of his car and raced toward her, shouting, "Your cat! Your cat!"

Thank the Good Samaritan

Apparently, Hutchinson's orange tabby (named Cuddle Bug) had been riding on the car's roof since she'd left home. They'd traveled almost 10 miles before the man on the highway flagged her down. Hutchinson finally unlocked her doors and thanked him. She also took Cuddle Bug home and, no doubt, strictly monitored his outdoor activities from then on.

First Felines

Residents of the White House have long shared their space with feline friends. Can you match the president to his cat(s)?

1. George W. Bush
2. Jimmy Carter
3. Bill Clinton
4. Calvin Coolidge

5. John F. Kennedy
6. Abraham Lincoln
7. Ronald Reagan

A. Tiger and Timmy. This president used to walk around the White House with Tiger around his neck and was so attached to the animal that when Tiger went missing, the president went on the radio to appeal for help finding him. Timmy allowed the president's canary to sleep between his paws.

B. Sara and Cleo. These tortoiseshell strays belonged to the president who was a former head of the Screen Actors Guild.

C. Socks. In 1991, this president and his family adopted Socks, a stray black-and-white kitten that they found in the garden of the soon-to-be first daughter's piano teacher.

D. Tom Kitten. This president gave Tom Kitten to his daughter, Caroline, who also kept a pony, a guinea pig, rabbits, and lambs at the White House.

E. Tabby. This president's son Tad was the proud master of Tabby.

F. India Willie. This president named his female cat after Texas Rangers player Rueben Sierra, nicknamed "El Indio." India Willie likes to play in the White House's West Garden Room, and her favorite things to eat are tuna-flavored treats.

G. Misty Malarky Ying Yang. This Siamese cat belonged to the daughter of the Democratic president who won the 2002 Nobel Peace Prize.

For answers, turn to page 221.

For the Record

There are a lot of amazing cats.
Here are some truly incredible ones.

Leo

Record: Longest Cat

Details: This orange-and-white Maine coon from Chicago weighs 35 pounds and is 48 inches long. Leo's owner, Frieda Ireland, says she has to watch Leo carefully while she's cooking because he's so big he will stand up, put his paws on the kitchen counter, and try to play by swatting the food onto the floor.

Towser

Record: Most Mice Killed

Details: For 21 years, this tortoiseshell tabby was in charge of rodent control at Scotland's Glenturret Distillery. Towser killed an incredible 28,899 mice in her lifetime. This feat so impressed the distillery's owners that, after Towser's death in 1987, they erected a statue on Glenturret's grounds to honor her.

Jake

Record: Cat with the most toes
Details: This orange tabby from Ontario, Canada, has seven toes on each paw, a total of 28! His owners, Michelle and Paul Contant, adopted Jake from a local humane society and said they knew when they saw him that he was special.

Anonymous California Spangled Cat

Record: Most expensive cat
Details: California Spangled cats are a rare breed that look like spotted wild cats. Most sell for $800 to $2,500. But in 1987, a California Spangled cat sold for $24,000. Both cat and owner remain anonymous.

Phet (a male part-Siamese) and Ploy (a female tabby)

Record: Most expensive cat wedding
Details: The kitties wed during a September 1996 ceremony in Thailand. They wore matching pink outfits, and the whole affair cost Wichan Jaratrcha (Phet's owner) $16,241.

Siberian Tiger

Cat: Largest member of the cat family

Details: The largest feline species is the Siberian, or Amur, tiger. In the wild, these cats grow to be about 8 to 10 feet long and generally weigh 650 to 675 pounds. In captivity, though, they have reached 13 feet in length and can weigh as much as 1,000 pounds.

Ragdoll

Record: Largest breed of housecat

Details: On average, ragdolls grow to weigh between 15 and 20 pounds. Their closest competitor is the Maine coon, which weighs an average of about 15 pounds.

Honorable Mention:

Florence Groff from France has the largest collection of cat memorabilia in the world. Groff began collecting in 1979, and by 2005, she had more than 11,000 cat-related trinkets, including 2,666 cat postcards, 2,070 cat figurines, 86 decorative plates, 48 refrigerator magnets, and nine lamps.

No More Wire Cages!

*Next time you go on vacation and have to leave
your cat at a kennel or pet boarder, consider one
of these posh "catotels" as an alternative.*

Bedfordshire, England

At the Miletree Catotel, about 40 miles northwest of
London, felines get the star treatment. Each cat gets his
own chalet, a carpeted room that pet parents can fill up
with kitty's favorite things from home. Especially pampered cats can book lakeside chalets, whose wide windows
overlook a tranquil duck pond (ducks included). And multiple cats from the same family can vacation together in a
family unit, which accommodates up to seven. Ruta and
Peter Towse started the catotel in the early 1990s as a
boarding facility for show cats. Over the years, it evolved
into a first-rate feline hotel for England's pampered kitties.

Arcadia, Australia

At the Calabash Kennels and Cattery in New South
Wales, Linda Meuman, Bob Hickman, and their staff
provide pets Down Under with quality care. The facility
opened in 1989, primarily as a luxury kennel for dogs.
But in 2004, Calabash expanded to include cats. And
include cats, they do! Calabash offers three types of kitty

accommodations: garden villas (rooms that allow cats to have 24-hour access to a private outdoor area full of tropical flora), balcony suites (rooms that include a sunny balcony where kitty can snooze), and garden view rooms (Calabash's standard rooms that face the outdoor play area). That play area is an elaborate, enclosed outdoor landscape with many logs and other things to climb; it also overlooks an open field where Linda Meuman's horses graze. There's an indoor play area too, complete with carpet-covered cat trees and sisal scratching posts.

Ottawa, Canada

In Ottawa, Melanie Walker runs the Pet Bed-and-Breakfast, a communal boarding facility. Here, kitty clients share a 2,500-square-foot maze of tunnels and play toys shaped like helicopters, Ferris wheels, trains, and roller coasters. Cats can also play with small floor toys and can rest or hide among the many plush cushions and hidey-holes. Sick, scared, or aggressive cats get private rooms. But all are welcomed by Walker's own feline trio: Moustacha, Sweet Pea, and Smudgie, who live at the B&B year round.

New York, New York

Catteries like those above will make sure your kitty experiences the good life, but Peter and Katie Lindenbaum, a father-daughter team in Manhattan, have come up with a new spin on the old cat-kennel routine. They've created a go-between service, called Katie's Kitty, that sets up cat parents in need of kitty-sitting with willing sitters. The Lindenbaums maintain a network of host families around the city who have been prescreened and approved. They introduce anxious parents to these families and even set up cursory play dates or overnight visits between host and sit-ee to make sure the two get along. Then, when the humans go on vacation, they'll know their cats are being cared for round-the-clock by a loving host family.

Posh Digs

Sitters and catotels aren't the only solutions for cat owners on the go. In the United States, traveling with a pet is more common than ever, and several posh New York City hotels have realized that the way to a human guest's heart is through his cat. The Starwood hotel chain in Manhattan offers feline guests turndown treats and cat-sized replicas of human beds. Loews hotels have a room-service pet menu formulated by a vet that offers gourmet appetizers and entrées (meat-eating, vegetarian, and vegan), milk, and bottled water. And Le Parker Méridien on West 57th Street has put together a special "Feed the Party Animal" menu that includes steak tartare. The cost? If you need to ask the price, you probably can't afford it—not that your cat cares what it costs you.

Famous Cat Lovers

*Behind every great man is a cat. Here's a look
at some historical figures and the cats they loved.*

Muhammad

This Muslim prophet adored cats, especially his tabby
Muezza. According to Islamic legend, Muhammad was
called to a meeting one day but did not want to wake up
Muezza, who had fallen asleep in his arms. So the prophet
cut off his sleeve and left it and the peacefully sleeping
Muezza behind.

Cardinal Richelieu

Before the 18th century, many Europeans considered
cats to be witches' familiars (a spirit that takes an animal
form), so it's odd that Cardinal Richelieu—a French
clergyman, statesman, and strident persecutor of witches—
would be a cat lover. But he was. Richelieu considered his
own cats to be free from sorcery, and he doted on them
throughout his life. He even gave them their own room in
his home. And for a man of the church, he chose a pecu-
liar name for one of his kitties: his black Angora was
named Lucifer.

Charles Dickens

According to his daughter, Mamie, Charles Dickens's animal of choice was the dog, but Williamina, a white cat who belonged to Mamie, seemed determined to change that. When Williamina delivered a litter of kittens, she brought them, one by one, to a corner of Dickens's study. Because the family had a collection of birds that lived in the house, the cats all lived outside, and Dickens instructed his daughter to take the kittens back outdoors. Mamie did, but Williamina continued to bring the kittens into the study, finally depositing them all at Dickens's feet. After that, he could no longer refuse her, and he allowed Williamina and her babies to stay in the house.

One of those kittens, a white cat who was nearly deaf, became Dickens's constant companion. The kitten was called simply the Master's Cat because he followed the master everywhere. One night, Mamie recalled, Dickens was reading in his study while the Master's Cat rested nearby. Tired of being ignored, the cat extinguished the reading candle with a swipe of his paw in an effort to get Dickens's attention. It worked. Dickens gave the kitty a pat and then went back to his book.

Edgar Allan Poe

In 1840, Edgar Allan Poe wrote an essay for *Alexander's Weekly Messenger*, a Philadelphia newspaper, in which he discussed his belief that animal instinct might be more powerful than human intelligence. One of the ways he

illustrated his point was to tell the story of his own black-and-orange cat Catarina and her ability to open locked doors. According to Poe, Catarina used her paws to force the door handle's thumb latch to release while she leapt at the door to push it open.

This smart kitty remained a revered member of Poe's household for many years. Catarina sat on the writer's shoulder while he worked, and in 1846, when his wife Virginia became sick with tuberculosis, Catarina often curled up at Virginia's side and purred.

Edward Lear

Famous for his limericks and whimsical art, this 19th century British author adored his tabby Foss, often rumored to be the inspiration for Lear's famous children's poem "The Owl and the Pussycat."

As he got older, Lear withdrew from public life and eventually retired to San Remo, Italy, where Foss was his only companion. The pair lived together in a villa on the Mediterranean Sea for almost 15 years before Foss passed away in November 1887. Lear buried his cat in the garden and then died himself two months later, in January 1888.

Theodore Roosevelt

America's 26th president loved the outdoors and had a deep respect for animals. He was especially fond of his gray cat Slippers, so named because the cat had an extra toe on each foot. Roosevelt was so enamored with his kitty that, one day, when Slippers was napping in a White House hallway, blocking a procession of diplomats returning from a state dinner, the president made a quick decision: everyone had to walk around the sleeping cat.

Winston Churchill

This World War II English prime minister had a pair of cats: Nelson (named after famed British sailor Horatio Nelson) and Jock. The two were beloved by their master, and Jock, in particular, always seemed to be at Churchill's side. The tabby attended cabinet meetings, and supposedly, dinner could not begin until the pampered pet joined Churchill at the table.

*   *   *

An average daily serving of dry cat food is equal to about five medium-sized mice.

Kliban's Cats

You may not know his name, but you've seen his cats.

Today, B. Kliban's plump, striped, googly-eyed, and colorful cats grace mugs, calendars, T-shirts, greeting cards, sheets, umbrellas, mouse pads—even doormats. His cat merchandise is a multimillion-dollar industry. But all this success took Kliban by surprise. Before publishing his breakout book, *Cat*, in 1975, he was just a reclusive artist living a beatnik lifestyle in San Francisco.

What Does the "B" Stand For?

Despite the fame of his creations, Kliban (pronounced KLEE-ban) remained a private person throughout his life. Biographical details are sketchy, but he did reluctantly reveal in a 1978 interview with the *New York Times* that the "B" in his name stood for Bernard, which he detested. Instead, friends knew him as Hap—short for Happy New Year—because he was born on New Year's Day 1935.

We also know that he grew up in Norwalk, Connecticut, was the son of Russian immigrant parents, and decided early on that he wanted to be a painter. He attended art school—first at Pratt Institute, then Cooper Union—but flunked out both times. After a few years of traveling around Europe, he motorbiked across the United States and landed in San Francisco, where he eked out a living doing odd jobs.

In 1962, Kliban became a regular cartoonist for *Playboy*. He also began selling comics to the *New Yorker*, *Punch*, *National Lampoon*, and *Esquire*. His comics for these publications were unique—one featured a woman fixing her lipstick in the mirrored sunglasses of a blind man—usually biting, and never featured cats.

Enter the Kitties

In 1974, Michelle Urry, Kliban's editor at *Playboy*, came by his apartment to look at some of his cartoons. While he hunted for his portfolio, she spotted some cat drawings Kliban had doodled while working on his latest *Playboy* submission.

Urry flipped through the cat cartoons—mostly portraits of Kliban's own cats—and thought they would make an excellent book. She set up Kliban with an agent, and the next year, New York's Workman Publishing printed *Cats*, a collection of cartoons and sketches. To the surprise of everyone, especially Kliban, it was a best seller.

Like Meatloaf, only Furry

Knowing they were onto a good thing, Workman pressed Kliban to draw more cats. The company created two calendars in the 1970s, both of which sold in the hundreds of thousands. Kliban also produced a few other books of cartoons, but none included his cats. Still, the calendars and first book had cemented his place in the American art world as a cat cartoonist.

As for how he felt about his most famous subjects, Kliban quipped that cats were "one hell of a nice animal, frequently mistaken for a meat loaf." He was also eager to point out that he was not a cat fanatic himself, saying, "I like them, but I'm not silly about them."

Cats out of the Bag

A few cat cartoons might not sound like groundbreaking art, but Kliban's cartoons have inspired other artists, most notably Gary Larson, creator of *The Far Side*. And Art Spiegelman (who won a Pulitzer Prize for his *Maus* books) credits Kliban with inventing the single-panel, third-person, caption-style comic that Larson made popular.

B. Kliban died in 1990, but his cats still make more than $10 million a year. Not bad for an art school dropout.

*   *   *

Cleopatra loved her kitty companion Charmian so much that the Egyptian queen designed her makeup to look like the cat's eyes.

Them's Fightin' Words!

*Kilkenny is a quiet hamlet in southeastern Ireland. It's also
the subject of a pugilistic English idiom. But how did
the town become associated with such a battle?*

One Cat Too Many?

The phrase "to fight like a Kilkenny cat" means to have a
no-holds-barred clash or, more commonly, to have two
people holding staunchly to different ideas and never finding any common ground. Most people agree that the
idiom came from the fighting felines in this anonymous
limerick:

> *There wanst was two cats in Kilkenny,*
> *Aitch thought there was one cat too many;*
> *So they quarreled and fit, they scratched and they bit,*
> *Till, excepting their nails, and the tips of their tails,*
> *Instead of two cats, there wasn't any.*

The origin of the limerick, however, is more
controversial.

Blame It on the French

Ask Kilkennians what the limerick is about, and you'll
get two theories. One has its foundation in Ireland's

contentious relationship with mainland Europe. Norman invaders (from what is now France) stormed Kilkenny in 1100 and took control of the town. They divided it into two districts: Irishtown and Englishtown, which housed Irish and English/Normans respectively.

The two groups disagreed so completely on politics that they were always at odds. Over time the bickering just got worse, and people from neighboring towns nicknamed them the "fighting Kilkenny cats" because they snarled and caterwauled like a pair of dueling felines. The cats of the limerick, say some residents, are metaphors for the bickering districts.

No, It Was the English!

A second explanation is more literal. English military general Oliver Cromwell invaded Ireland in 1650. While he and his men camped near Kilkenny and awaited military action, some of the soldiers got bored and went looking for entertainment. They found it in two cats whom they tied together at the tails, strung over a clothesline, and watched fight each other.

When one of the commanding officers got wind of the fracas, he demanded the men put a stop to it. So the soldiers cut the cats free, leaving the animals' still-bound tails behind. But the officer saw only the tails on the line and deduced that the cats fought to the death, leaving behind only the tips of their tails—hence the legend in the limerick.

Koko Kares for Kitten

A kitten and an ape change how we think about gorillas.

Scientists still wonder whether animals can reason the way humans do. It's an age-old debate, with recent evidence indicating that intelligence and the ability to feel emotion aren't limited to humans. Weighing in heavily (about 300 pounds) on the side of animals is Koko, the famous signing gorilla.

Learning to Speak Human

In 1972, Francine "Penny" Patterson was a young graduate student in psychology at Stanford University when she met Hani-ko, a one-year-old female gorilla at the San Francisco Zoo, and began teaching her sign language. Within two weeks the gorilla, nicknamed Koko, was signing for food and juice. Project Koko became the longest continuous attempt to teach language to another species.

Today, Patterson states that Koko has a vocabulary of more than 1,000 signs in American Sign Language and can understand 2,000 words. The gorilla has participated (with human help) in a live e-mail chat on AOL and has conversed with famous folks like presidential speechwriter Peter Forbes, Apple CEO John Scully, and celebrities like

William Shatner and Robin Williams. Other animals have since learned to sign, but few are celebs like Koko, whose initial rise to fame was linked to mothering a kitten named All Ball.

Koko's Kitten

Among young Koko's favorite toys were books with pictures of cats. In 1984, Koko signed to Patterson that she wanted a cat. As an experiment, abandoned kittens were brought to the gorilla compound, and Patterson let Koko choose one for a pet. The gorilla picked out a round, gray male kitten with no tail and named him All Ball.

Koko mothered All Ball in devoted gorilla fashion. She tried to nurse him and carried him on her back, imitating the way gorilla mothers carry their babies in the wild. When she wanted to play with All Ball, Koko often signed the word "tickle," and she would gently tickle the cat.

The Ron Cohn photo "Koko and Kitten" shows Koko cradling All Ball. Though her large arms could crush the seemingly helpless kitten, she cuddled him carefully and gazed at him fondly. That photo surprised the public, who was fascinated by the gentleness of a supposedly ferocious animal. Koko's mothering of All Ball won her millions of admirers.

Koko in Mourning

Tragedy struck in December of 1984, when All Ball escaped from his enclosure and was killed by a car. Koko seemed distraught and signed words like "cry," "sad," and "frown" when shown a picture of a kitten that looked like hers. Disagreement raged in the scientific community over whether or not Koko could actually grieve for her lost kitten and feel emotions in the same way that people do. Despite the arguments, the public had no trouble believing that Koko could feel a mother's pain and loss. Expressions of sympathy and offers to replace All Ball with another kitten poured in from around the world.

All Ball's Legacy

Koko's reaction to All Ball's death and her ability to communicate those emotions sparked more research and heated debate about behaviors once considered exclusively human. Today, she stands as a diplomat for the gorilla community, once believed to be bloodthirsty. Koko's maternal side and sadness at the loss of her kitten made many people rethink traditional ideas of what it is to be human and what it is to be animal. Perhaps there is more going on than we think.

Since All Ball's death, Koko has cared for two other cats: a gray kitty called Smoky and an orange Manx named Lipstick.

Cats and Dogs

"If animals could speak, the dog would be a blundering outspoken fellow, but the cat would have the rare grace of never saying a word too much."

—*Mark Twain, author*

"If a dog jumps into your lap it is because he is fond of you; but if a cat does the same thing it is because your lap is warmer."

—*Alfred North Whitehead,*
British philosopher

"You call to a dog and a dog will break its neck to get to you. Dogs just want to please. Call to a cat and its attitude is, 'What's in it for me?'"

—*Lewis Grizzard, author*

. . . And Pigs

"I like pigs. Dogs look up to us. Cats look down on us. Pigs treat us as equals."

—*Winston Churchill, former*
British prime minister

Ads All Folks

*For nearly a century, advertisers have employed
spokes-cats to sell products. Here are some of the felines
who have made their brands famous.*

Tony the Tiger

In 1952, Kellogg's execs planned to feature a menagerie of
animals—one for each letter of the alphabet—on packages of its Sugar Frosted Flakes cereal. They started with
E (Elmo the Elephant), K (Katy the Kangaroo), N (Newt
the Gnu), and T (Tony the Tiger). But they never got
any further. Tony was so popular that in 1953, he became
the cereal's official spokes-character and the others were
abandoned.

Tony's image has changed over the years. He used to
walk on all fours and sport faded orange-and-black stripes.
Today he stands on two legs, and his stripes are black and
bright orange. Also, in the first Frosted Flakes commercials, Tony was invisible—except to kids who ate his
cereal—but now Flakes-eaters, parents, and anyone who
watches TV can see him. Even with all these changes,
though, one thing remains the same: his voice. Tony's
growl belongs to Thurl Ravenscroft, an ex-radio star who
jokingly claimed to have made a career out of just one
word: "Grr-reat!"

Sainte Cat

Every summer since 1980, thousands of music fans have gathered at the Montreal International Jazz Festival to hear their favorite jazz artists perform live. They also get to see the festival's official mascot, Sainte Cat, on billboards, T-shirts, posters, and stage sets.

Sainte Cat is a cartoon drawing of a thin blue cat wearing sunglasses, usually playing an instrument or curled up in the shape of a music note. The festival's organizers came up with the logo because they felt the cat best exemplified the laid-back, cool feel of jazz and blues music. The name Sainte Cat is also a play on words: it's the abbreviated name of Rue Sainte-Catherine, Montreal's main downtown drag and the road where many of the festival's major outdoor concerts are staged.

Morris the Cat

In 1968, Bob Martwick of the Leo Burnett advertising agency (the company responsible for such advertising icons as the Jolly Green Giant and the Pillsbury Doughboy) rescued Morris (née Lucky) from an Illinois animal shelter and turned him into a star. That year, the agency created an ad campaign for 9Lives cat food that revolved around a finicky, spoiled feline who ate only one kind of food: 9Lives, of course. The admen wanted the cat to be in charge of his household and his humans, but not to be overly aristocratic; he had to be an every-cat. Lucky, a 15-pound orange-striped tabby with green eyes, fit the bill.

Lucky reigned as Morris the Cat until his death in 1975. After that, two other Morrises succeeded him and continued to keep the cat (and the cat food) in the public eye. In 1972, Morris starred in a movie called *Shamus*. During the 1980s, he penned (pawed?) three books. And in 1988, he made a bid for president (but lost to Vice President George Bush).

Puma

Rudolf and Adolf Dassler, German brothers with an interest in athletic shoes and sportswear, formed a company called Adidas in the 1920s. But in 1948, the brothers had a falling-out, so Rudolf left Adidas and Adolf behind to start his own brand: Puma. He chose a silhouette of the leaping jungle cat as his logo.

This clothing and shoe line quickly became popular with stars in all types of sport. And over the years, some of the world's most impressive athletes have donned Puma gear, including Jesse Owens, Pelé, Marcus Allen, Martina Navratilova, and Serena Williams.

Jaguar

In 1935, another big cat reached the heights of luxury and decadence when the Jaguar became the symbol of a high-end automobile. Use of the jaguar name and imagery was intended to illustrate the car's elegance, and it worked. For many people, the Jag's sleek lines and silver hood ornament in the shape of a leaping cat conjure up images of class and sophistication. But it comes with a steep price. The least-expensive Jaguar (a sport sedan called the X-Type) starts at about $33,000. And for $75,000+, you can own one of the coolest cats on the block: the Jaguar XK.

The Esso Tiger

If you're looking to fill up your Jag, you might want to "put a tiger in your tank" courtesy of Esso Oil, an international subsidiary of ExxonMobil. This popular gasoline company has been using its distinctive tiger mascot in ads since 1936, when the animal first pitched Ethyl Motor Oil in England.

Yet, despite this long history, the Esso tiger didn't reach the height of his popularity until the 1960s, when advertisers softened his traditionally ferocious appearance, recast him as a cartoon character, and launched a media blitz that made Esso Oil famous. Esso offered bumper stickers (proclaiming "I've got a tiger in my tank!") and orange-and-black-striped tiger tails at its gas stations all over the United States. By the time the ad blitz was through, more than 2,500,000 tiger tails had been sold. *Time* magazine proclaimed 1964 "the year of the tiger"—the Esso tiger, that is. And the big cat even inspired a 1965 Buck Owens tune, "I've Got a Tiger by the Tail."

The Meow Mix Cat

Anyone who owns a cat knows just how vocal they can be, especially at mealtime. That fact became the premise for Meow Mix cat food, the product that "tastes so good, cats ask for it by name!" Meow Mix cats have been singing the praises of this popular food in a variety of commercials since the 1970s by whining the catchphrase, "Meow, meow, meow," ad nauseam.

Despite their popularity, the now-famous ads are actually a product of serendipity. During the filming of a Meow Mix spot in 1972, a cat accidentally began choking on the food. Filming continued but the animal repeatedly opened and closed its mouth until the food dislodged. After seeing the footage, Meow Mix ad executives were inspired to insert a simple song to give the illusion the cat was singing rather than gagging. So, in a strange twist, a near-fatal accident became part of pop culture.

*   *   *

Chauvet Cave in southern France is home to the world's oldest cave paintings and carvings, created about 35,000 years ago. Much of the artwork depicts animals, and the most prominently featured is the cat. There are 74 images of lions in the cave and one of a leopard, showing that the oldest cultures on earth clearly interacted and had a relationship with big cats.

Cat Capers, Part 2

*Our stories of ordinary cats who found fame
continue. (Part 1 is on page 66.)*

Headline: *Cat Makes Weather Forecasters Look All Wet*
The Feline Star: Napoleon
What Happened: In the summer of 1930, a severe
drought hit Baltimore, Maryland. Forecasters predicted
an even longer dry spell, but Frances Shields called local
newspapers and insisted they'd have rain in 24 hours. The
reason? Her cat Napoleon was lying down with his "front
paw extended and his head on the floor," and he only did
that just before it rained. Reporters laughed . . . until there
was a rainstorm the next day.
Aftermath: Newspapers all over the country picked up the
story, and Napoleon became a feline celebrity. He also

became a pro-
fessional
weather-
cat and
newspaper
columnist.
His predic-
tions were

printed regularly—and he did pretty well. All told, he was about as accurate as human weather forecasters.

Headline: *World Gets Charge from Nuclear Kittens*
The Feline Stars: Kittens Alpha, Beta, Gamma, and Neutron, who were living at the San Onofre nuclear power plant near San Diego, California
What Happened: How do you make a nuclear power plant seem warm and fuzzy? Find some kittens there. In February 1996, just as the owner of the San Onofre power plant was kicking off a pro-nuclear PR campaign, a worker happened to find four motherless kittens under a building. A pregnant cat, the story went, had slipped through security at the plant, given birth to a litter of kittens, and disappeared. When the worker tried to carry the kittens off the grounds, alarms went off. It turned out that the cute little animals were slightly radioactive—though officials explained that they were in no danger. The story was reported worldwide. The *Nuclear News*, a nuclear industry publication, called it "the biggest nuclear story in years."
Aftermath: Seven months later, the Atomic Kittens were pronounced radiation free. Offers to adopt them flooded in from all over the world, but workers at the plant decided to take the kittens home themselves.

*   *   *

Calico cats are almost always female.

Hollywood Cats

*Any cat owner knows that all cats demand the star treatment
from their humans. But some felines actually head to Hollywood
(or have trainers who bring them there) and make it in the
movies. Here are five of the most memorable movie
kitties from the last four decades.*

Cat, *Breakfast at Tiffany's* (1961)

Truman Capote once said that Holly Golightly in
Breakfast at Tiffany's was his favorite creation. For the most
part, Cat, Holly's feline friend, would probably agree. Cat
lives a free and pampered life with Holly in her New York
apartment. The pair is separated briefly when Holly
(played by Audrey Hepburn) tosses Cat out in the rain
during an argument. She quickly realizes her mistake and
rescues the kitty, but Hepburn, an animal lover, said later
that performing the tossing scene was among the most
"distasteful things" she'd ever had to do in a movie.

Feline actor Orangey played Cat and won a Patsy award
(the animal Oscar) for his work in *Breakfast at Tiffany's*.

Milo, *Milo and Otis* (1986)

This orange-and-white cat and his canine pal (a pug
named Otis) are best friends who grow up together on the
same English farm. The pair gets into several pickles

(including battling a hedgehog over a chicken egg Otis was supposed to be babysitting), but the film takes a scary turn when the two are separated during a play session. Milo ends up floating downriver in a wooden crate while Otis follows along the bank. Bears, waterfalls, and other perils lie ahead, but the friends aren't willing to give up on each other.

Milo and Otis was based on a Japanese movie called Koneko Monogatari (or, The Adventures of Chatran).

Sassy, *Homeward Bound* (1993)

Appropriately named, Sassy is a Himalayan cat who, accompanied by two canine companions, sets out to find her human family after the trio mistakenly believes they've been left behind (the humans actually left the animals with friends only temporarily). The animals face both man-made and natural obstacles on their long journey home and must cross the Sierra Nevada mountains before they can be reunited with their owners. Homeward Bound is a remake of the similarly themed The Incredible Journey, released in 1963. The film also inspired a 1996 sequel called Homeward Bound II: Lost in San Francisco, in which the trio forsakes the countryside for the wilds of the city.

Mr. Bigglesworth, *Austin Powers: International Man of Mystery* (1997)

A central character in the first Austin Powers film, Mr. Bigglesworth belongs to Dr. Evil, Austin's archenemy. Bigglesworth was once a fine Angora kitty with beautiful white fur, but after a mishap with a cryogenic freezing technique, the cat lost all his hair and turned into a hairless sphynx. The inspiration for Mr. Bigglesworth was another silver-screen feline: Solomon, the white Persian who belonged to Ernst Stavro Blofeld, one of the villains in the James Bond film series.

Crookshanks, *Harry Potter and the Prisoner of Azkaban* (2004)

Before he was a movie star, Crookshanks was a literary darling, the feline sidekick of Harry Potter's good friend Hermione Granger. In the movies, as in the books, Crookshanks is a fluffy, orange cat with a flat face. He appears in several *Harry Potter* installments, but his most important contribution occurs in the third film, *Harry Potter and the Prisoner of Azkaban*, when he tries to out Ron Weasley's rat as an evil wizard in disguise. Author J. K. Rowling explained that she modeled Crookshanks after a haughty ginger cat she knew in London who had a face so flat it looked like the animal had run into a wall. The cat appeared to lack any social hang-ups related to his condition and thus seemed a perfect pet for the spunky Hermione Granger.

Decode Your Cat's Chatter

*Cats are among the most vocal house pets around.
Here, Uncle John explains kitty's two most
common communication techniques.*

Meows

A cat's meow is definitely his preferred vocal communication method. Cats meow to convey many different ideas and emotions, and they expect their owners to be able to decipher a request for food from a warning. So pay attention.

- **"Feed Me" Meow:** This is a persistent attempt to capture the owner's attention. Some cats even lead their owners to their food bowls and continue to meow until they have been filled.

- **"People Food" Meow:** Usually a high-pitched wail, cats often use this meow when their humans are eating. Kitties like to be included at all mealtimes, and even if they ultimately turn up their noses at what their owners are serving, they like being able to pick and choose.

- **"You Left Me"**
  Meow: This plaintive
  cry alerts owners
  whose kitties have
  been left alone for too
  long. It also doubles as
  the "open that door"
  meow for cats whose
  humans have inadver-
  tently (because who
  would do it on pur-
  pose?) closed a door—
  any door—in the cat's
  house.

- **"Here I Am" Meow:**
  A cat in a dark room
  sometimes sounds this warning because cats would
  rather announce their presence than get stepped on.

- **Silent Meow:** Chattering teeth devoid of sound mean
  that the cat has spotted a potential prey and is prepar-
  ing to pounce. All birds, mice, chew toys, toes, and
  strings of yarn should flee immediately.

Hissy Fits

The second most common kitty communication technique
is the hiss. Many owners assume this is just a show of

general irritation, and that's not far off. But most cats have different levels of hissing that show increasing displeasure.

- **"Stay Away" Hiss:** This is a quick expulsion of air, usually directed at dogs or other interlopers trying to prevent kitty from doing what she wants.

- **"I'll Fight Ya" Hiss:** A longer hiss, usually accompanied by a predatory stance. This hiss warns that an attack is forthcoming.

- **Caterwaul:** Not technically a hiss, the caterwaul often follows hissing in a cat argument. This howling scream can come just before or in the midst of a fight. Some cats, however, skip the hissing stage altogether and go straight to caterwauling in an effort to rebuke intruders.

* * *

In 1760, a book called *The Life and Adventures of a Cat* was published in England. The main character was a "ram" cat (as male cats were known back then), named Tom the Cat. The book was so popular, though, that ever since, males have been known as "tomcats."

Purrr-fect Bed Warmers

*Cat lovers on the go enjoy a special treat at the historic
Anderson House hotel. Not only does the bed-and-breakfast offer
quaint, old-style rooms, but it also allows travelers to choose one
of its in-house kitties to keep them company for the night!*

Since 1856, the Anderson House hotel in Wabasha,
Minnesota, has provided weary visitors with a warm,
inviting atmosphere and vintage charm. The rooms are
adorned with high-backed beds, handmade quilts, marble-
topped dressers, antiques, and pictures from the Victorian
era. To keep guests' feet warm at night, hotel staffers
deliver a hot brick in a quilted envelope to each room.
And the dining room offers menu items that have been
served there since at least 1920, including chicken soup
with homemade noodles, cinnamon rolls, and double
Dutch fudge pie.

The Stars of the House

But what really makes the Anderson Hotel unique are the
residents of Room 19: the Cat Room. There, five cats
stretch, play, and work on looking cute. The friendliest
feline is Ginger; she loves attention. Morris is sweet and
sociable, too. Goblin purrs up a storm, and Arnold is kid-
friendly. The newest kitty, Aloysius, is shy but loving.

Guests who hate to travel without their pets (or who wish they had a kitty at home) may borrow one of these felines each night of their stay, free of charge.

Cats have been stars at the Anderson House for more than 30 years. Former owner John Hall says his mother, Jeanne, was an avid cat lover. She helped him run the place during the 1970s, and one hotel guest so loved Jeanne's cat that Jeanne lent the guest the cat during his stay. After that, cat sharing became so popular at the Anderson House that the hotel now loans a cat to one in every five visitors. John Hall notes that the kitties "are as common as a bucket of ice would be in other hotels."

Borrowing a Cat for the Night

Here's how it works: First, guests decide which cat they'd like. The current owners, Teresa and Mike Smith, can help steer travelers toward an appropriate companion, depending on what they're looking for. For example, small children and fast movements startle some of the cats. Morris doesn't like to be picked up, and Ginger can be overactive at night. The Smiths take these things into consideration before choosing a guest's temporary pet.

After dinner, visitors return to their rooms to find their kitties waiting for them. Because travelers generally neglect to pack a litter box, cat food, water dish, and cat toys, those are delivered to the room as well. The traveler and kitty then keep each other entertained for the night, and the cat just might purr its newfound friend to sleep. No wonder the Smiths call the cats the "purrr-fect bed warmers"!

Guests who are allergic to cats or are otherwise cat-avoidant can choose cat-free rooms. And visitors are welcome to bring their own small pets to stay with them at the inn, although anyone planning to adopt a cat for the night should probably leave Tweety or Rover at home.

* * *

An Inspired Tale

The Anderson House cats inspired a 1997 children's book called *Blumpoe the Grumpoe Meets Arnold the Cat*. This story tells the tale of a grumpy old man named Horace P. Blumpoe who stays at the Anderson House. Arnold, the only cat who hasn't been chosen to stay with a guest that night, sneaks into Blumpoe's room and so captures the old man's heart that Blumpoe asks for Arnold to be his companion during his next visit to the Anderson House.

Getting in a Flap

*Everyone knows about Sir Isaac Newton's contributions
to mankind, but what about those he made to feline-kind?*

Mew Oughta Know

The ancient Greek philosopher Plato once said,
"Necessity is the mother of invention." That was certainly
the case for 17th- and 18th-century English physicist Sir
Isaac Newton, who invented the cat flap to help his pet
cat Spitface pass freely from one room to the next.

The idea for the cat flap came to Newton while he was
tinkering in his attic laboratory. He was working in the
secluded room while he conducted experiments on the
behavior of light. These experiments required darkness
(hence, the attic location), but his beloved kitty wouldn't
leave him alone. When Spitface
wanted Newton to let her into
his laboratory, she nudged open
the door with her nose, allowing
outside light to filter in. This
ruined Newton's experiments. It
also presented him with a problem: how could he indulge his cat
while still conducting his tests?

Putting an Idea in Motion

After giving the matter some thought, Newton came up with a solution. He hollowed out the bottom of his attic door and covered the hole with a piece of felt. This simple design allowed Spitface to come and go as she pleased while also keeping the integrity of her master's experiments intact.

Purr-fecting the Concept

Over the years, the cat flap's design has been improved. The use of sturdier, weather-resistant materials makes modern cat flaps more durable than Newton's original felt and wood design. Some companies have also introduced electromagnetic catches that link to a magnet embedded in an animal's collar. This feature ensures that the flap opens only for the pet who lives in a particular house. And cat flaps aren't just for cats anymore. Dog owners use the flaps (often called doggy doors) to give their canines free access to their backyards. But no matter the advances that flood the marketplace, pets around the world are indebted to Sir Isaac Newton (and Spitface), who opened doors for millions of animals.

*   *   *

"Meow is like aloha—it can mean anything."

—Hank Ketchum, cartoonist, creator of Dennis the Menace

Cat Tales

Legends of cats with mysterious powers have been around for thousands of years. Nearly every culture has at least one. Here's some feline folklore that's been passed down over the centuries.

Bast

The ancient Egyptians began worshiping this cat-headed goddess more than 5,000 years ago. Her name means "devouring lady" and she was worshiped in temples throughout Egypt—especially on October 31, Bast's Feast Day. Bast was said to be the daughter of the sun god Ra and was associated with the moon, music, dancing, mother-hood, and violent vengeance. In the Egyptian Book of the Dead, she was said to destroy the bodies of the deceased with her "royal flame" if they failed entry tests for the underworld. Out of respect for Bast, the Egyptians staged expensive funerals for cats, during which gold and gem-studded cat figurines were buried along with the mummi-fied body of the deceased kitty.

El Broosha

The ancient myths of the Sephardic Jews (Hebrews who left Israel and went to what is now Spain and Portugal) tell of Lilith, Adam's first wife who was created before Eve. According to the legend, when Lilith refused to submit to

Adam, she was banished from paradise. But Lilith continued to haunt the earth as a demon in the shape of a huge black vampire-cat named El Broosha (or sometimes El Brooja—*bruja* means "witch" in Spanish) who sucks the blood of newborn babies.

Freya

In Norway, this Viking goddess of love and fertility kept cats as pets and rode in a chariot pulled by two winged cats that were the size of horses. Freya was among the Vikings' most popular goddesses, and the cats she loved were also adored by Norse societies. Norwegian brides often received kittens as wedding gifts to symbolize the giver's wish that the bride and her husband have a happy life together and bear many children.

Grimalkin

Its name comes from its color (gray) and *malkin*, an archaic word for cat. Scottish legend tells of a wraith called a grimalkin: a human by day, a fierce wild panther roaming the Highlands by night. The huge gray cat has magical powers; it can also appear in the form of a hare and can disappear at will. During the Middle Ages, the grimalkin—and cats in general—became associated with the devil and witchcraft. Women tried as witches during the 16th, 17th, and 18th centuries were often accused of having a "familiar," a devilish companion animal. What kind of animal? Usually a grimalkin.

Jaguar Sun

The Maya of Central America worshiped a cat god called the Jaguar Sun, who rose each day in the east and journeyed west. After the sun set, the cat god had to fight lords of the underworld all night. But he always won the battles and rose again in the morning. In honor of the sun god, Mayan warriors wore jaguar skins to help them in battle, and shamans were said to be able to shape-shift into the big cats.

Li Shou

Li Shou was a cat goddess worshiped by the ancient Chinese. They believed that at one time cats had the ability to speak, but they gave the gift to humans so that the cats could lie around all day. Li Shou was a fertility goddess who brought rain and protected crops. At harvest time, peasants held a festival in her honor and offered sacrifices to the cats who protected the grain from rats.

Matagot

According to European folklore, matagots are magical cats. The French say that a matagot can be lured home with a plump chicken. If people treat the animal well once it's in the house, he will bring good luck. For example, give the matagot the first bite of every meal, and he will reward you with a gold coin each morning. And in England, people whispered that Dick Whittington, a humble boy who grew up to become mayor of London during the 15th century, owed his good luck to his matagot.

*   *   *

A Night on the Town

In New York City, you can do a lot with your pets: take your dog for a walk in Central Park or partake of the numerous dog and cat spas in the city. And now, thanks to Meow Mix cat food, you can also take your kitty out for a meal.

The Meow Mix Café opened on 5th Avenue in 2004, and cat lovers all over the city rushed to try it out. The Café offers foods to delight both feline and human patrons: mackerel for kitties, tuna rolls for people. And the house rule is easy to follow: No dogs allowed!

Kit Lit

*Think you know the cats featured in children's literature?
Here's your chance to prove your stripes.*

1. What's the name of the cat who kept company with
good old bulldog Jack in Laura Ingalls Wilder's *Little House
in the Big Woods*, the first novel in her *Little House* series?
   A. Black Susan
   B. Pet
   C. Jill

2. After the three little kittens lost their mittens, what
treat did Mother Cat threaten to take away from them?
   A. Cream
   B. Cake
   C. Pie

3. In what Marguerite Henry novel does a cat named
Grimalkin befriend a Moroccan stable boy and a cham-
pion stallion?
   A. *Misty of Chincoteague*
   B. *Black Gold*
   C. *King of the Wind*

4. What is the name of Alice's pet cat, featured in Lewis Carroll's *Alice in Wonderland* and *Through the Looking Glass?*

    A. Cheshire Cat

    B. Dinah

    C. Salty

5. Crookshanks belongs to which of Harry's friends in the *Harry Potter* series by J. K. Rowling?

    A. Neville Longbottom

    B. Hermione Granger

    C. Ron Weasley

6. In the C. S. Lewis novel *The Lion, the Witch, and the Wardrobe,* Aslan the lion sacrifices himself for the sake of Narnia at the hands of which character?

    A. The White Witch

    B. The Ice Witch

    C. Jadis the sorceress

7. In which author's poem did the pussycat and the owl sail together in a beautiful pea-green boat?

    A. Rudyard Kipling

    B. Edward Lear

    C. Hans Christian Anderson

8. Tom Kitten, a naughty young cat in Beatrix Potter's *The Tale of Tom Kitten*, had two siblings. What are their names?

A. Tim and Tam

B. Flopsy and Mopsy

C. Moppet and Mittens

9. The warrior cats Tigerstar and Fireheart are both characters in a popular contemporary series by which author?

A. J. K. Rowling

B. Lemony Snicket

C. Erin Hunter

10. Which March sister kept kittens in Louisa May Alcott's *Little Women?*

A. Jo

B. Beth

C. Meg

For answers, turn to page 221.

*   *   *

"A home without a cat, and a well-fed, well-petted and properly revered cat, may be a perfect home, perhaps; but how can it prove its title?"

—*Mark Twain, author*

Reunited

These cats prove that, sometimes,
you really can go home again.

Sneakers

In 1996, one-year-old Sneakers the cat disappeared from his
Seattle, Washington, home. His owner, four-year-old Hilary
Keyes, was devastated. He was her first pet, a long-haired
black cat with green eyes who loved to curl up in her lap to
watch TV. Hilary, her six-year-old sister, and their mother
canvassed the neighborhood looking for Sneakers. They put
up flyers, went door-to-door, and called local shelters, but
found nothing except the cat's collar left behind in their
yard. The family reluctantly gave up on Sneakers, and
Hilary eventually got three other cats.

But then, in 2006, Hilary received an unexpected phone
call. An administrator at an animal shelter in Sacramento,
California, had found Sneakers. A local couple had dropped
him off, saying they could no longer care for him, and the
shelter employee tracked down Hilary and her mother after
scanning Sneakers for a microchip. No one knows how
Sneakers ended up so far from home—the family that
dropped him off hadn't offered any explanation. But Hilary
and her family, although shocked by the discovery of their

long-missing pet, welcomed him with open arms. After 10 years, Sneakers made one more journey . . . back to Seattle and onto the lap of 14-year-old Hilary Keyes.

Tiger

In July 2004, the Valentino family was moving from Hawaii to Arizona. They packed up their cat, Tiger, in a carrier and loaded him into the cargo hold of their United Airlines flight. Just before the plane took off, however, United employees discovered that Tiger had escaped. They searched the cargo hold, but to no avail—the cat was gone. The Valentinos were crushed. They continued on to Arizona but stayed in touch with United and airport officials who were on the lookout for Tiger. Six weeks later, an airport employee spotted a black and brown striped cat outside one of the airport buildings. The employee caught the animal, who was still wearing his collar, and brought him inside. The next day, after a hearty meal and good night's sleep, Tiger boarded a United flight

for Arizona. This time, the kitty flew first class (in a securely locked carrier) and was reunited with the Valentinos in Phoenix.

Cupcake

When Hurricane Katrina devastated New Orleans in 2005, many residents were forced to evacuate without their pets. Tristan Carter, a former New Orleans resident who moved to Atlanta, Georgia, after the storm, was one of those. Carter lost a lot in the hurricane: her grandfather, her home, her dogs, and her rabbit. And she thought she'd lost her black cat, Cupcake, too.

But six months after Carter fled New Orleans, she got a call from a volunteer for Animal Rescue of New Orleans, a group that airlifted food and water to homeless animals left in the city after the storm and worked to reunite pets with their families. After an extensive search, the volunteers located Carter in Atlanta. With Cupcake found, Carter acknowledged that even though black cats have a reputation for bringing bad luck, Cupcake is actually her "good luck charm."

Baby

In February 2006, arsonists destroyed a Brooklyn, New York, apartment building. Five-year-old Mekhi Dowman and his mother made it out alive, but their orange tabby, Baby, was nowhere to be found. Mekhi's mother was sure Baby had succumbed to the flames and smoke, but Mekhi wasn't ready to give up. He kept reassuring his family that Baby would be fine. Two months later, he was proved right, when Baby was found in the care of New York City's ASPCA. A fire marshal had turned Baby over to the shelter after discovering the animal on a staircase inside the burned building. Veterinarians treated Baby for burns, and then ASPCA officials enlisted the help of the Red Cross to find the Dowmans.

As soon as they got the call, Mekhi and his mother went to the shelter in Manhattan where the cat was being held, and the boy and his pet were reunited. As for how they'd spend their first night together, Mekhi said they would watch Batman cartoons, play with a ball, and when Baby got hungry, he'd offer the cat "what he likes to eat—cat food. Nice, tasty cat food!"

* * *

A Real Crowd Pleaser

In 1904, a New York City man sprinkled catnip powder on the pavement, attracting hundreds of cats. When a policeman arrested him for being a public nuisance, the cats followed cop and prisoner all the way to the precinct headquarters, where the night watchman spent the entire night trying to shoo them away. The catnip culprit was released in the morning (along with his horde of four-legged followers), and all charges were dropped because there are no laws against entertaining neighborhood cats.

His Purr-fect Name

*The 30 most popular male cat names in the
United States . . . Where does your cat rank?*

1. Max
2. Tigger
3. Tiger
4. Smokey
5. Oliver
6. Simba
7. Shadow
8. Buddy
9. Sam
10. Sammy
11. Charlie
12. Simon
13. Oscar
14. Lucky
15. Jake

16. Sebastian
17. Jack
18. George
19. Rocky
20. Bailey
21. Toby
22. Milo
23. Buster
24. Leo
25. Rusty
26. Oreo
27. Gizmo
28. Felix
29. Chester
30. Harley

Her Purr-fect Name

The most popular female cat names . . .

1. Chloe	16. Jasmine
2. Lucy	17. Patches
3. Cleo	18. Sasha
4. Princess	19. Gracie
5. Angel	20. Precious
6. Molly	21. Daisy
7. Kitty	22. Shadow
8. Samantha	23. Ginger
9. Misty	24. Sassy
10. Missy	25. Lily
11. Sophie	26. Bella
12. Baby	27. Abby
13. Maggie	28. Smokey
14. Zoe	29. Annie
15. Callie	30. Tigger

The Cyprus Cat

*When it comes to keeping domesticated cats, scientists
have long believed that the ancient Egyptians led the way.
However, a Frenchman excavating on the Mediterranean
island of Cyprus made a discovery linking cats to a culture
that predates the Egyptians by thousands of years.*

Dating feline domestication is tricky, say most
scientists, because an animal's leap from wild to tame
is likely a lengthy process. But nearly everyone agrees that
the ancient Egyptians lived with tame cats. Egyptian art
and writings confirm that cats were a big part of the culture, and thousands of cat mummies have been found in
Egyptian tombs.

Because cats were such a big part of Egyptian society
and no solid evidence of tame cats in other cultures
existed, archeologists deduced that ancient Egypt was the
first culture to domesticate cats. In 2001, though, French
archeologist Jean-Denis Vigne offered a different opinion.

Buried Treasure

In 1992, excavations began at Shillourokambos, the oldest
Stone Age settlement on Cyprus. Nine years later, Vigne
and his team unearthed a cat skeleton near a human burial
plot. The human bones were about 9,000 years old (meaning

they were buried more than 4,000 years before the Egyptians first kept cats as pets). And although Vigne and his team couldn't date the cat's bones because they were too degraded, several clues led them to believe that the cat and human had been interred together.

Clue #1: The cat's bones showed no signs of abuse. This indicates that the animal had not been part of a ritual sacrifice.

Clue #2: The cat was buried only about 15 inches from the human, whom Vigne assumes to be its owner.

Clue #3: The burial plot seems to spread out several feet around the human and feline remains. Near the skeletons, Vigne and his team found polished stones, tools, jewelry, and 24 complete seashells (such shells were prized by ancient cultures), and they believe that these items were buried with the human and the cat.

These clues led Vigne to believe that the human-feline pair had been carefully laid to rest in the same plot and, thus, that they were also companions in life.

The Dissenters

Not everyone agrees with Vigne's theory, of course. He has many critics who argue that the 15 inches separating the Cyprus cat and the human remains don't necessarily imply a connection. These scientists afford less weight to the theory that the burial plot spreads out over several feet. They argue that the Cyprus cat was removed from the human and, therefore, wasn't as important to the Cypriots as domesticated animals were to other cultures (ancient Egyptians, for example, who buried cats and humans together). Critics also cite evidence that dogs, domesticated as many as 12,000 years ago, were so beloved by their masters that they were often buried alongside them. Not so the Cyprus cat.

There's no consensus yet, and scientists continue to study the finds at Shillourokambos. But Vigne is sticking to his theories and continues his digs on Cyprus in the hopes of finding more to substantiate his claim.

* * *

The cat found at the Cyprus site is a *Felis silvestris*, a species of African wild cat that scientists believe is one of the ancestors of the modern housecat.

* * *

"In the beginning, God created man, but seeing him so feeble, He gave him the cat."
—*Warren Eckstein, animal trainer*

Catnip Crazy

*Even if you know all about catnip's intoxicating effects on felines,
here are five catnip facts you may not know.*

1. Catnip is a member of the mint family, and its scientific
name is *nepeta cataria*.

2. Europeans and Asians long used catnip to treat everything from fevers and flatulence to nervousness and morning sickness. English colonists brought catnip to North
America because of its medicinal uses, and it now grows
wild over most of the continent.

3. Catnip affects only about two-thirds of cats (though no
one knows why), and susceptibility seems to be an inher-
ited trait. Geriatric cats and kittens younger than three
months old don't seem to be affected by it at all.

4. Catnip has been used to trap mountain lions because
many big cats are particularly susceptible.

5. A study at Iowa State University suggests that nepeta-
lactone, a chemical in catnip, is 10 times more effective at
repelling mosquitoes than DEET, the chemical used in
almost all insect repellents.

The Lyin' King

We've unearthed this tale in an effort to puzzle out who really came up with the idea for The Lion King.

Inspiration

In 1950, a Japanese artist named Osamu Tezuka created *Jungle Taitei* (*Jungle Emperor*), a story about an orphaned lion cub who is destined to rule the animals in Africa. From 1950 to 1954, it was a Japanese comic book series, and in 1965, Tezuka turned it into Japan's first color animated television series. The following year, all 52 episodes were released in the United States under the name *Kimba the White Lion*. Over the next few years, Kimba enjoyed some success in syndication, mostly on local or regional TV stations, and Tezuka acknowledged that the work of Walt Disney—*Bambi* in particular—was an inspiration for the story of his lion hero.

In 1994, nearly 30 years after the creation of Kimba and five years after Tezuka's death in 1989, Disney released its feature-length animated film *The Lion King*—about an orphaned lion cub destined to rule the animals in Africa.

False Pride

Officially, the executives and animators at Disney denied they had ever even heard of Kimba. But fans of the original *Kimba the White Lion* were incensed over the many similarities they found between the two projects. A group of more than a thousand animators in Japan sent a petition to Disney asking the studio to acknowledge its debt to the original series. Disney refused, citing only *Bambi* and Shakespeare's play *Hamlet* as influences. Walt Disney reportedly met Tezuka at the 1964 World's Fair in New York and mentioned that he someday hoped to make something similar to Tezuka's earlier creation, *Astro Boy*. But Disney died in 1966, 28 years before *The Lion King* was made. If he were really a fan of Tezuka's work, would he have approved of the project?

Copycat

Some of the most striking similarities between *The Lion King* and *Kimba the White Lion* include the following:

- The main characters' names are remarkably similar: Simba and Kimba.
- Both are orphaned as cubs and destined to become rulers. Each loses his father under tragic circumstances.
- In *The Lion King*, Simba turns to a wise but eccentric baboon (named Rafiki) for guidance. In *Kimba the White Lion*, Kimba turns to a wise but eccentric baboon (named Dan'l Baboon) for guidance.
- One of Simba's friends is a hysterical yet comical bird (named Zazu). One of Kimba's friends is a hysterical yet comical bird (named Polly).

- Simba has a cute girlfriend cub named Nala. Kimba has a cute girlfriend cub named Kitty.
- Simba's chief nemesis is Scar, an evil lion with a scar over his left eye. Kimba's primary nemesis is Claw, an evil lion with a scar over his blind left eye.
- In *The Lion King*, Scar enlists the aid of three hyenas (Shenzi, Banzai, and Ed). In *Kimba the White Lion*, Claw enlists the aid of two hyenas (Tib and Tab).
- Kimba and Simba each speak to the spirit of their fathers; both father-spirits appear in the clouds.
- The image of Simba as a grown lion standing on Pride Rock in *The Lion King* is almost identical to an image of Kimba as a grown lion standing on a jutting rock surveying his kingdom in *Kimba the White Lion*.

Catfight

Disney may have "borrowed" the idea, but they were legally protected. Mushi Productions, the company that made *Kimba the White Lion*, went bankrupt in 1973 and U.S. rights to the show ran out in 1978. That means *Kimba* was in the public domain.

* * *

"If man could be crossed with a cat it would improve man, but it would deteriorate the cat."

—*Mark Twain, author*

Chartreux and Sphynx

*One has French flair, one has no hair . . . our discussion of breeds ends
with two that have noticeably different styles when it comes to coats.*

A Holy Order

The big, sturdy Chartreux, with its gray-blue fur and yellow or copper eyes, is one of the world's oldest cat breeds.
As far back as 1558, poet Joachim du Bellay noted that
natural colonies of "entirely gray" cats were common in
France. Eighteenth-century naturalists Linnaeus and the
Comte de Buffon also made mention of this "blue cat of
France," and the writer Denis Diderot referred to a
Chartreux in his first novel, *Les Bijoux Indiscrets (The
Indiscreet Jewels)*, in 1748.

Although monastery records no
longer exist to confirm the story, legend has it that beginning in the 16th
century, Chartreux cats lived with an
order of French monks known as
Carthusians. The breed took its name
from the monks' abbey house in
Grenoble, the *Grand Chartreux*.
Chartreux are quiet cats—some people
say they took the monks' vow of

silence. And Chartreux sometimes sit up on their hind legs and raise their front paws in front of their chests in a gesture akin to praying.

Vive Le Chat!

The wide-eyed Chartreux, with its dense, woolly coat and a mouth that appears to be smiling, became a patriotic symbol during World War II, when the writer Colette opted to remain in Paris with her Chartreux companions throughout the German occupation. Colette's novel *La Chatte* revolves around a Chartreux cat—a "little bear with fat cheeks and golden eyes"—who is so beloved by her fictional master that his new bride is made terribly jealous. Charles de Gaulle, leader of the French resistance fighters battling the German occupation, also owned Chartreux cats.

The war decimated France's Chartreux population. Postwar breeders reported that few of the pedigreed animals survived and that no known natural colonies existed at war's end. But postwar breeding programs in France, England, and the United States brought the Chartreux back. Although still rare, the cat is now well established in Europe and North America.

Canadian Hairless

Some cats have long, thick fur. Others have soft, smooth coats. And then there's the sphynx, with no hair at all—or none to speak of, anyway.

The only pedigreed cat from Canada, the sphynx traces its ancestry to 1966, when a house cat in Toronto gave birth to a hairless kitten. This kitty, and others that arose elsewhere as a result of the same mutation, formed the breed's foundation.

Wrinkly and big-eared, the sphynx is not actually bald, but covered with a peach-fuzz down. Owners report that the sphynx makes a loving and entertaining pet and say the animals are well suited for most people who are allergic to cat dander, although even a sphynx can trigger an attack in those who are severely allergic.

Suave and Suede

Easy as they are to get along with, sphynx cats need a little extra TLC. Because they lack fur coats, sphynxes get cold more easily than standard cats and enjoy finding snuggly spots under the bedcovers or being tucked in with a hot water bottle; some owners even buy them sweaters. Moreover, the sphynx's lack of fur does not mean easy care. With no hair to absorb body oils, the sphynx's skin—which has been compared to suede or chamois in look and feel—needs regular bathing.

These soft-skinned cats became especially popular during the late 1990s, when a suave sphynx named Ted Nude-Gent played Mr. Bigglesworth, Dr. Evil's cat, in the Austin Powers series. The cats became so popular that in 1998, the Cat Fanciers' Association accepted them for registration and competition. Despite its newfound popularity, the sphynx remains a rare cat, and breeders report that there's usually a waiting list for kittens.

* * *

Peppermint Prevails

In the 1980s, Peppermint was living a life of leisure. The white cat had a doting young owner and spent most of her days lounging in the sunshine near her home in Melbourne, Australia. But Peppermint also had a past. Ten years earlier, she'd lived in the medical laboratory of Australian researcher Struan Sutherland, who was trying to find an antivenom for the bite of a Sydney funnel-web spider. Often called the deadliest spider in the world, the funnel-web can kill a small child in 15 minutes, but Sutherland had heard that cats were immune. No one had proved it, so Sutherland decided to test the theory on Peppermint. He gave Peppermint five doses of funnel-web spider venom and then waited. But nothing happened. That amount of venom would most certainly have killed a human, but it had no effect on Peppermint.

Sutherland perfected his antivenom in 1980, and since then, no one in Australia has died from a funnel-web bite. But neither he nor the researchers who followed him were ever able to find out exactly what in the cat's physiology protected her from the venom. Peppermint might consider it just good luck, but more likely, she'd deem it one more bit of evidence that cats are indeed the superior species.

Maneki Neko

This cat has long been considered a symbol of good luck in Japan and other Asian countries.

The Beckoning Cat

If you've ever walked into a Chinese or Japanese business and noticed a figure of a cat with an upraised paw, you've met Maneki Neko (pronounced MAH-neh-key NAY-ko), the "Beckoning Cat." She is displayed to invite good fortune, a tradition that began with a Japanese cat many centuries ago.

According to legend, that cat, called Tama, lived in a poverty-stricken temple in 17th-century Tokyo. The temple priest often scolded Tama for contributing nothing to the upkeep of the temple. Then one day, a powerful feudal lord named Naotaka Ii was caught in a rainstorm near the temple while returning home from a hunting trip. As the lord took refuge under a big tree, he noticed Tama with her paw raised, beckoning to him, inviting him to enter the temple's front gate. Intrigued, the lord decided to get a closer look at this remarkable cat. Suddenly, the tree was struck by lightning and fell on the exact spot where Naotaka had just been standing. Tama had saved his life! In gratitude, Naotaka made Tama's temple his family temple and became its benefactor. Tama and the priest never went hungry again. Tama lived a long life and was buried at the temple, renamed Goutokuji temple. Goutokuji still exists, and it houses dozens of statues of the Beckoning Cat.

Lucky Charms

Figures of Maneki Neko became popular in Japan during the 19th century. At that time, most brothels and many private homes had a good-luck shelf filled with lucky charms, many in the shape of male sexual organs. When Japan began to associate with Western countries in the 1860s, those charms began to be seen as vulgar. In an effort to modernize Japan and improve its image, Emperor Meiji outlawed the production, sale, and display of phallic talismans in 1872. People still wanted lucky objects, however, so the less controversial Maneki Neko figures became popular.

Eventually the image of the lucky cat spread to China and then to Southeast Asia. How popular did the Beckoning Cat become? In Thailand, the ancient goddess of prosperity, Nang Kwak, was traditionally shown kneeling with a money bag on her lap. Now she's usually shown making the cat's raised-hand gesture and occasionally sporting a cat's tail.

Maneki Neko Facts:

- Sometimes Maneki Neko has her left paw up, sometimes the right. The left paw signifies that the business owner is inviting in customers. The right invites in money or good fortune.

- Most Maneki Nekos are calico cats because the male calico is so rare it's considered lucky in Japan. But Maneki Neko may also be white, black, red, gold, or pink. These colors supposedly ward off illness, bad luck, or evil spirits and bring financial success, good luck, health, and love.
- Maneki Nekos made in Japan show the palm of the paw, imitating the manner in which Japanese people beckon. American Maneki Nekos show the back of the paw, reflecting the way we gesture, "Come here."
- The higher Maneki Neko holds her paw, the more good fortune is being invited.
- Hello Kitty, a popular toy character in Japan and the United States, was inspired by Maneki Neko.

* * *

This Dog's the Cat's Meow

In 2005, participants at the Westchester Cat Show in New York attended a special memorial service. Showmen (both human and feline) gathered to hear the eulogy of Ginny, a Siberian Husky mix dog who was a savior of cats. Ginny once dug through a box of broken glass to rescue a cat buried inside, and she spent several years working with rescue teams to find lost or injured kittens. In 1998, the folks at Westchester named her Cat of the Year, so eulogizing her after her death seemed appropriate. The service was a solemn affair for the heroic dog who spent so much of her life trying to help her feline brethren.

Purr Me a River

We wondered . . . why do cats purr?

For most cat lovers, the dulcet tones of a feline purring mean the kitty is happy. Much of the time, that's true. But experts suggest that those same noises can also mean other things. In particular, there are three primary theories about the purr.

Purr-fectly Stressed Out

Sure, a cat purrs when she's on your lap being petted, but did you know she'll also do it when you take her to the vet or when she's in any tense situation? According to some scientists, the reason cats do this is that their purring is self-soothing, and the vibrations may help them calm down.

Other animal experts argue that purring in stressful situations is a form of communication for the cat—it may indicate submissiveness to a perceived attacker or may be an effort to get the predator to back off. The communication hypothesis derives from the fact that purring frequencies have been recorded between 25 and 150 hertz, indicating that cats might be controlling purring levels to convey different messages.

Cat, Heal Thyself!

Another theory suggests that the vibrations created by purring actually keep cats healthy. Purring may, some researchers say, help cats to retain bone density, ward off muscle atrophy, and maintain good blood circulation. Because cats evolved to remain inactive for long periods of time in order to conserve energy between hunts, the animals needed a passive method to stimulate their bones and muscles. Enter the purr: a low-energy way for cats to keep themselves fit without too much running around.

Mommy's Rumbling

The purr is also a way for a mother cat to call her kittens to feed. Because kittens cannot see, hear, or smell very well when they are newborns, their mother's purring acts as a vibration that homes the kittens in to where they can find milk. And, because newborn kittens purr instead of meow (they begin meowing after a couple of days), their purring reassures the mother that her babies are healthy.

Laws of Nature

Here are just a few of the cat-related statutes that have been made law in the United States.

To Protect the Public

In Destin, Florida, any cat who terrorizes pedestrians is officially deemed a "bad cat." And this isn't just a simple case of name calling. Owners of bad cats can be slapped with a $100 fine.

The citizens of Columbus, Georgia, like their sleep. Cats aren't allowed to yowl after 9:00 p.m.

Your cat needs a taillight to roam the streets in Sterling, Colorado.

In Topeka, Kansas, each household can have no more than five felines.

For the Birds

In Cresskill, New Jersey, cats must wear three bells to announce their presence to neighborhood birds.

In Reed City, Michigan, you can't own a cat and a bird at the same time.

Saving Kitty's Litter

One of our favorite tales of feline bravery:
Scarlett the cat nearly died—not once, but
five times—saving her kittens from a fire.

A Near Cat-astrophe

The scrawny calico cat was living the hardscrabble existence of a stray in a gritty neighborhood in Brooklyn, New York. She would have remained one of the thousands of nameless stray cats had it not been for her heroic actions on March 29, 1996. On that day, the calico had been tending her five kittens, born just four weeks before, when the abandoned garage in which she'd made her home suddenly burst into flames.

As the fire raged, firefighters were shocked to observe the plucky mom, though seriously burned herself, repeatedly brave the inferno—emerging each time with another of her kittens. She carefully placed each kitten just outside the door before going back for the next. When all five were safely outdoors, she began taking them, one by one, across the street, farther away from danger.

At four weeks old, the kittens could never have survived the blaze had it not been for their mother's loving attention. But the mother cat was severely injured. Her eyes were blistered shut and she could not see. The pads of her paws were scorched, and her ears and nose were singed. There were bare patches on her face and body where the fur had been burned off.

Rescuing the Rescuer

David Gianelli was one of the firefighters on duty the night of the garage fire. An animal lover, he was touched by the little cat's courage and determination. As soon as the fire was contained, he found a cardboard box and gently transported the mother and her kittens to the North Shore Animal League on Long Island. During the trip, the calico cat kept touching each of the kittens in turn. Even though she couldn't see them, she seemed to be counting them to make sure they were all right.

By the time they reached their destination, the mother cat was barely alive and two of her kittens were in bad shape. The doctors at the Animal League worked feverishly to save them. League workers named the brave little mother Scarlett after the red patches of skin showing where the fur had burned away.

Scarlett needed oxygen to breathe, intravenous antibiotics to fight infection, drugs to combat shock, and antibiotic ointments for her skin. Despite the odds, she began to improve within a couple of days of constant care. When the swelling around her face subsided, she was able to open her eyes. Eventually, the tips of her ears had to be amputated, but her recovery from the ordeal was deemed miraculous.

Only one of the kittens succumbed to pneumonia as a result of smoke inhalation. The others made a full recovery.

A Famous Feline

News of Scarlett and her daring rescue spread quickly as tales of her bravery were featured on numerous news broadcasts and television talk shows. The North Shore Animal League was deluged not only with local requests for news and offers to adopt Scarlett and her kittens but also with queries from around the world, as far away as South Africa and Japan. With more than 1,500 adoption offers, Marge Stein, manager of public relations at the Animal League, held a contest to find Scarlett and the kittens the best home.

A Purr-fect Ending

From the thousands of entries they received, the Animal League selected Karen Wellen to be Scarlett's owner. Wellen had written of her great empathy with the cat. Having survived a car accident that left her with a slight disability, Wellen felt that she and Scarlett had much in common.

Scarlett soon moved to Wellen's Brooklyn apartment, a far cry from the gritty streets she used to know. She gained weight and thrived under Wellen's attentive care. Scarlett's four surviving kittens were also adopted by loving families in New York.

Scarlett's Honors

Even after her adoption, Scarlett continued to be honored. In 1999, the IAMS pet food company named Scarlett the "top cat of the century," after she won 29 percent of the online vote. On September 19, 2000, she won the first Scarlett Award for Animal Heroism, which was named after her. The award-winning cat has even had two books written about her.

Perhaps the most touching tribute of all came on May 12, 1996, when the *New York Daily News* printed part of a poem composed by one of Scarlett's many admirers. The poem is titled "The Heroine," and reads, in part, as follows:

Why is everyone so surprised that I saved my furry five
That in spite of pain and danger, I brought them out alive…
Every trip was a burdened choice but I could make no other
The rescuers have called me cat, but I am also mother.

The MGM Lion
By the Numbers

This big cat has become one of the most recognizable animals on the silver screen. Take a look at his long career by the numbers.

In 1921, Samuel Goldwyn, soon-to-be co-owner of the Metro-Goldwyn-Mayer (MGM) movie studio, met animal trainer Volney Phifer and his lion, Slats, whom Phifer had brought to the United States from Africa several years before. Goldwyn was so impressed by the lion's long mane and commanding appearance that he decided to use the animal as the logo for his company's movies. Christened "Leo," the lion has appeared before every MGM movie ever since.

1
Song that inspired the lion logo as MGM's trademark. The tune was "Roar, Lion, Roar," Columbia University's fight song.

3
Number of times Leo roars in the logo: one short, one long, and one short.

5

Number of different lions who have appeared on the MGM trademark: Slats, Pluto, Tanner, Jackie, and an unnamed lion who appeared in 1957 but was quickly fired because he growled too much. Tanner is the one most moviegoers are familiar with. He appeared before all of MGM's Technicolor films during the studio's golden age (1938–1956).

12

Television shows that feature Mimsey in a parody of the MGM lion logo. This orange kitten is the trademark for MTM (Mary Tyler Moore Enterprises), and he first appeared on the small screen in the 1970s at the end of the *Mary Tyler Moore Show*. The kitten meowed (instead of roared) to close the program. The Mimsey trademark also appeared on 11 other television shows produced by Mary Tyler Moore Enterprises during the 1970s and 1980s.

50 tons

Weight of the bronze Leo statue that welcomes visitors to the MGM Grand Hotel and Casino in Las Vegas. Sculpted by artist

Snell Johnson, the Las Vegas Leo stands 45 feet tall, is 50 feet long, and is made up of 1,660 pieces of bronze welded together.

197 Morristown Road

Address in Gillette, New Jersey, where the original Leo is buried. Trainer Volney Phifer moved to a farm in the 1930s and boarded animals there. When Leo I (a.k.a Slats) died in 1936, Phifer buried the animal on the property and marked the spot with a block of black granite and a pine tree. The property changed hands many times over the next 60 years, and in 1996, the owners removed both the stone and the tree when they cleared the yard.

1928

Year MGM added the lion's roar to its trademark. MGM started using the lion trademark as early as 1924, but in those days, films were still silent and accompanied only by music. On July 31, 1928, Leo roared for the first time before the movie *White Shadows of the South Seas*, MGM's first talkie. The roar belonged to Pluto, the second feline actor to play Leo and the first to record his roar.

*   *   *

Cats have no collarbone, so they can fit through any opening the size of their heads or larger.

Home Sweet Home

*It all began with a seven-foot-tall scratching
post covered with 395 feet of red sisal.*

In 1986, when Bob Walker and Frances Mooney (artists,
authors, and cat lovers) moved into their San Diego,
California, home, they wanted to give their cats a special
place to play. So they put up a floor-to-ceiling post in the
living room, wound sisal around it, and figured their kitties
would be thrilled. They were. But Walker and Mooney
noticed that the cats tore through the house and raced up
the post, only to come to a staggering halt when they saw
the ceiling. That seemed like an unnecessary dead end, so
the couple decided to expand.

Cats in the Wall

What they've cre-
ated in the years
since is the ulti-
mate feline-friendly
home. Raised cat-
walks, spiral stair-
cases, ramps, and

162

holes between walls are the norm. The couple's eight cats lounge above the living room, bedroom, dining area, hallway, and kitchen, resting in flame-shaped nooks or on carpeted ramps. They even have their own cat hideout built above a hall closet. The area (complete with caged toy mice hanging from the ceiling) is where the kitties can escape when they're tired, frightened, or just plain sick of human company.

Walker and Mooney have also incorporated the 140 feet of cat paths into their décor. The house and walkways are painted in bright colors: orange, purple, red, and pink. And cat memorabilia—everything from teacups to lamps to a painting Mooney describes as "gravel-by-numbers"—decorate most of the 1,500-square-foot home. The kitchen floor is even an homage to kitties: Mooney covered the floor with a collage of cat pictures from magazines and then lacquered them onto the tile. It's a cat paradise because, as Walker says, "If possession was nine-tenths of the law, it would really be their house." Yeah, they know.

Walker, a professional photographer, even documented the building of the unusual house in his witty and colorful book, *The Cat's House*.

* * *

The most primitive ancestor of modern cats is believed to be the now-extinct miacis, a small mammal who made its home in trees and lived 45 to 50 million years ago.

West Versus Midwest

Two felines compete for the title of "world's smallest cat."

The Incumbent: Mr. Peebles

Hometown: Pekin, Illinois

Birthdate: April 2002

Height and Weight: 6.1 inches tall; 3.1 pounds . . . so small he fits into a standard size dinner glass.

Story: In 2004, Donna Sassman, a veterinarian in Illinois, made a routine visit to a local farm. She had been called out to vaccinate several dogs. While there, Sassman noticed a small brown and white tabby kitten stumbling among several larger cats. The little kitty seemed overwhelmed by his larger housemates and Sassman worried that he would be trampled or, worse, would suffer malnutrition because he wasn't able to fight the bigger cats for a turn at the food bowl. So Sassman asked the owner if she could have him. The response was, "Sure . . . if you can catch him."

After several tries, Sassman managed to scoop up the kitten. She loaded him into her car and took him home. When she got him to her veterinary clinic in Pekin, she discovered something extraordinary: the kitten was not a kitten at all. He was a two-year-old munchkin cat.

Munchkin cats are the result of a genetic mutation. Their heads are a normal size but their bodies and legs are shorter. As Sassman examined her new kitty, she began to wonder how many others were as small as he was or if other cats his size even existed. She certainly hadn't seen any. So Sassman christened the little guy "Mr. Peebles" after a ventriloquist's dummy on a *Seinfeld* episode and wrote to the people who compile the *Guinness Book of World Records* to find out if her cat was indeed a candidate for the record books.

A packet of information soon arrived, and Sassman diligently went to work filling out the 10-page application. She submitted photos of Mr. Peebles along with the paperwork and then had him examined by two Guinness-approved veterinarians. Shortly thereafter, Sassman received word that Mr. Peebles did indeed qualify for the title of World's Smallest Cat. He beat the previous record holder (a cat named Itse Bits) by only two-tenths of a pound!

Guinness plaque in paw, Mr. Peebles (accompanied by Sassman) hit the media circuit. He appeared on *Good Morning America*, was featured in a *National Geographic* children's magazine and the *National Enquirer*, and was the subject of an Associated Press release. By early 2004, Mr. Peebles was a bona fide celebrity, and it seemed he wouldn't be pushed off his throne any time soon.

But then came the news from California.

The Challenger: Heed

Hometown: Portrero, California

Birthdate: January 2006

Height and Weight: 3.5 inches tall; 2 pounds . . . so small he can hide behind a Coke can.

Story: Mr. Peebles has stiff competition in a black-and-white kitten from Portrero, California. Named Heed (because a Scotsman declared upon seeing the newborn kitten, "Look at the heed on that lil' guy"), this little fellow beats Mr. Peebles's record by about a pound. Granted, Heed is still a kitten and will probably grow a little bit more, but he's so tiny that his veterinarians and owner, Tiffani Kjeldergaard, don't think it will be much.

Like Mr. Peebles, Heed is a munchkin cat, though his pedigree isn't pure: his mom is a munchkin, and his dad is a regular-size feline. But the kitten's small size isn't holding him back. Heed already has his own Web page and has met with agents at a Los Angeles–based talent agency. Most importantly, though, the *Guinness Book of World Records* has taken an interest in him. So Mr. Peebles had better enjoy his *Guinness* crown while he can—it appears there's a brand new kitten in town, and he's poised to take the title.

* * *

The first official cat show was held in England in 1871.

Things Cats Should Never Eat

Here's a list of the 10 worst foods for cats.

1. What kitten doesn't love a saucer of milk? But believe it or not, most cats are lactose intolerant. Milk products may give them diarrhea, which can lead to dehydration or other serious problems.

2. You might think your cat craves chocolate the same way you do, but chocolate can be poisonous to felines. It contains theobromine, an alkaloid that, in cats, can cause arteries to constrict, heart rate to increase, and the central nervous system to fail.

3. The average tabby is likely to turn up her nose at onions, a good thing since the odiferous vegetable can be fatal to cats. Chemicals in onions can damage red blood cells, which in turn can cause anemia and breathing difficulties. Garlic and other root vegetables have similar chemicals and are also harmful to cats.

4. Because cats are carnivores, it might seem natural to give them raw meat—but don't do it. Salmonella bacteria form quickly on raw meat and poultry, and this can cause an intestinal disorder. Raw meat can also harbor parasites that sometimes lead cats to contract toxoplasmosis (a disease that can damage the brain, eyes, or other organs).

5. Whether you pronounce it toe-may-toe or toe-mah-toe, don't give it to your cats. Tomatoes contain an alkaloid that, although harmless to humans, can be poisonous to cats.

6. Cartoon cats may eat fish in one gulp and leave only the skeleton behind, but don't risk giving your cat anything with bones. Meat and fish bones are potential choking hazards. They can also splinter after being digested and become lodged in kitty's intestines. Even large bones are dangerous, because cats can actually break their teeth trying to chew them.

7. Raw egg whites contain an enzyme called avidin that prevents the absorption of biotin in the intestines, a deficiency that can lead to skin diseases in adult cats and growth problems in kittens. A little cooked egg every now and then is OK, though.

8. Cats, like other animals, are attracted to food by its smell. So even though they probably would not relish the taste of coffee or alcohol, the strong, pleasant odors might tempt your kitty to take a sip or two. Caffeine and alcohol deplete the body of important vitamins and minerals, though, and can cause liver damage in cats.

9. She may be a natural predator, but don't let your cat eat mice. The large doses of pesticides and poisons an average rodent is likely to have ingested can be toxic to your cat. Fortunately, most cats don't eat mice anyhow. They just leave the rodents next to your shoes as an offering.

10. Although your kitty may howl for tuna, don't give in to her demands very often. Eating too much tuna can result in a vitamin B_1 deficiency, which in turn can lead to heart problems. B_1 deficiency also robs cats of vitamin E, which can lead to skin diseases.

Warning!

Never give your cat aspirin, ibuprofen (Advil), or acetaminophen (Tylenol). Although helpful to humans, these drugs can be fatal to cats.

This information was compiled from a variety of sources but isn't medical advice. If your cat has any health problems, be sure to consult your veterinarian.

Liger Love

The movie Napoleon Dynamite *introduced many people to the liger, Napoleon's favorite animal. Uncle John was surprised to learn that this creature, which seemed to be straight out of mythology, actually exists.*

A Swimming Hybrid

A liger is a cross between a male lion and female tiger. These felines can be gargantuan, the true kings of the forest. Measured from nose to tail tip, the average liger stands 12 feet tall and weighs approximately 1,000 pounds. And you thought your cat was fat!

Ligers take after their parents in a number of ways. They have their mother's stripes and their father's tawny, golden coloring. They roar like lions, swim like tigers, and, in the case of male ligers, often have manes (albeit sparse ones).

A Rare Sight

If you've never seen a liger, you're not alone. There are only about a dozen of these creatures worldwide, and all of them are in captivity. The scarcity of ligers is due in large part to the fact that lions and tigers inhabit different territories. Lions prefer open grasslands such as those found in Africa, whereas tigers favor thick forests or areas with tall grass, such as those found in India. In fact, the only time the two giant cats do intermingle is in zoos and animal sanctuaries, where they often share the same enclosure.

This close proximity has been responsible for the some-times deliberate, but mostly accidental, breeding of lions and tigers for more than 50 years. Although no one is certain where the first liger birth occurred, one leading candidate is Utah's Hogle Zoo, which unexpectedly became home to a liger named Shasta on May 14, 1948.

Literary Ligers

In spite of their rarity, or perhaps because of it, ligers have become a part of pop culture. In addition to being Napoleon Dynamite's favorite creature, ligers have appeared in the television program *Transformers Cybertron*, the comic book series *Warheads*, and in the Irvine Welsh novel *Marabou Stork Nightmares*. In most cases, these representations focus on the animal's immense size, casting them as powerful warriors with otherworldy powers.

Liger Facts:

- The flip side of a liger is a tigon, a cross between a male tiger and a female lion. Unlike ligers, tigons tend to be smaller than both of their parents, tipping the scales at a mere 350 pounds. Generally speaking, tigons are also rare, due to male tigers' natural aversion to mating with female lions.
- Lions and tigers aren't the only breeds of big cats to mate successfully. Zoologists have also created leopons (a cross between a male leopard and a female lion) and lepjags (a jaguar-leopard mix).

- Napoleon Dynamite may claim ligers as his favorite animal, but the drawings he does of them don't resemble the actual hybrid. Instead, Napoleon's sketches look more like a manticore, a creature from Persian mythology that has a man's head and a lionlike body. A manticore is a fearsome beast that has horns, gray eyes, red fur, and a scorpion's tail.

* * *

Cats on the Cover

According to publishers, cat-themed books and books with cats on their covers sell better than most others. One publisher even says that if she can work a cat into a book's cover design, she'll sell 25 percent more copies.

So it's no surprise that several cat-themed titles are available today:

- Author Lilian Jackson Braun's "The Cat Who . . ." is a series of mystery titles that feature felines Koko and Yum Yum as title characters.
- Rita Mae Brown authors a series called "Sneaky Pie" that is "co-written" by her cat Sneaky Pie.
- Carole Nelson Douglas writes the "Midnight Louie Mysteries," in which feline Midnight Louie and his human companion solve mysteries.

The Tom and Jerry Story

The cartoon world's most famous cat and mouse are more than 60 years old. But with cable TV airing their cartoons daily, a whole new generation knows (and apparently loves) them.

In the late 1930s, MGM had a full-time animation studio. But as Disney and Warner Brothers cartoons became more popular each year, MGM's list of cartoon flops kept growing. One reason was its disorganized and indecisive management. Another was weak characters; MGM had nothing to compete with Bugs Bunny or Mickey Mouse.

William Hanna and Joe Barbera, two young MGM animators, were convinced that the studio would soon fold, so they decided they might as well develop a cartoon of their own. After all, what did they—or MGM—have to lose? They picked a cat and mouse as their subjects because, as Joe Barbera put it, "half the story was written before you even put pencil to paper."

Don't Call Us . . .

In 1940, they finished *Puss Gets the Boot*, about a cat named Jasper who tries to catch an unnamed mouse. The brass at MGM didn't care for it, but since they didn't have anything else in the works, they released it to theaters. To their surprise, the public loved it. The cartoon was even nominated for an Academy Award.

It was just what MGM needed. So Hanna and Barbera were shocked when MGM executives called them in and told them to "stop making the cat and mouse cartoons." Why? Because they "didn't want to put all our eggs in one basket."

"Of course," Barbera says wryly, "before *Puss Gets the Boot*, MGM didn't have a single good egg to put in any basket." But orders were orders, and the men halted production. Shortly after, however, MGM got a letter from a leading Texas exhibitor asking, "When are we going to see more of those adorable cat and mouse cartoons?" The Texan was too important to ignore, so Hanna and Barbera were given the green light to develop the series.

What's in a Name?

Now that the men were going to make more cat and mouse cartoons for MGM, they needed names for their characters. Instead of painstakingly researching and developing a title for the pair, Hanna and Barbera asked fellow workers to put pairs of names into a hat. The pair they picked: Tom and Jerry. An animator named John Carr won 50 dollars for the name idea. MGM made millions.

For 17 years, Hanna and Barbera, still unknown to the public, made more than 120 Tom and Jerry cartoons in the basement at MGM. Because the lead characters didn't talk, the cartoons' success depended on top-notch animation and writing that relied heavily on facial expressions and timing. Composer Scott Bradley's musical scores for each cartoon held all this together. Ultimately, the Tom and Jerry cartoons won seven Academy Awards. Due to financial constraints, however, the studio dropped the series in 1958. Hanna and Barbera went on to create their own animation studio and churned out more made-for-TV cartoons than anyone in history, including *The Flintstones*, *The Jetsons*, *Yogi Bear*, and *Scooby-Doo*.

Meanwhile . . .

In 1963, five years after the last Tom and Jerry cartoon was made, Warner Brothers animator Chuck Jones moved to MGM to resurrect the series. Not only did he have the unenviable task of toning down the violence in a cartoon that revolved around it, but by Jones's own admission, he didn't understand the characters. What came out was a wimpy cartoon that didn't have the flair of the previous Tom and Jerry series. The plots and animation were static, and Scott Bradley's carefully constructed scores were replaced by stock 1960s music. After three unsuccessful years, MGM dropped the cat and mouse for good.

Since then, the series has been resurrected for TV in a number of different varieties (like *Tom and Jerry Kids*) by Hanna-Barbera Studios.

Hooray for Hair Balls

*Most people believe that a hair ball is exactly that . . . a ball of hair.
That's mostly true, but there is a little bit more to its construction.*

A Trich of the Bezoar

The scientific term for a hair ball is *trichobezoar*. These
masses of hair begin with the cat's natural grooming
process. When your kitty licks her fur, she inevitably swal-
lows some of her own hair. Some of this passes naturally
through her system. But some hair stays in her stomach.

When enough hair accumulates in the animal's belly, a
hair ball forms. This usually happens anywhere from one
to four times a month. And even though all cats develop
hair balls, long-haired breeds
tend to have more frequent
episodes due to the natu-
ral density of their fur.

The Cat Can Hack It

Veterinarians and animal
physiologists have studied
hair balls for decades.
They've analyzed the gooey masses

and discovered that hair balls contain hair, obviously, but also undigested fat, ash from food products, and mucus resident in a kitty's stomach and esophageal tract. These materials bond tightly with the hair and grow ever bigger until a hair ball forms that needs to be expelled from the cat's body. The hair ball then triggers a vomiting mechanism, and the cat expels the mass. If the animal didn't have this natural expulsion urge, a hair ball could kill her because it would block the passage of food or get stuck in her stomach, intestines, or esophagus.

A cat expelling a hair ball can be an unsettling sight. The animal usually coughs or gulps and looks like she's choking. But really, there's no need to be alarmed. The noises are usually followed by the delivery of the offending hair ball. And your kitty will be better off for having purged the tangled mess.

* * *

Fighting Hair Balls

There are several products on the market that pet owners can give their cats to help hair balls pass through the kitties' systems (thereby avoiding the whole hacking mess). Most of these are petroleum jelly–based and flavored with tuna, chicken, or beef. Your veterinarian can recommend the product best suited to your particular animal.

Nine Lives, Part 2

Read about more amazing cat rescues. (Part 1 is on page 43.)

From Peugeot to Purr-geot

A stray kitten in Glamorgan, Wales, found a warm place to sleep—under the hood of a taxicab. When the cab's owner discovered the cat, it took more than an hour to coax the animal out from under the hood. When the kitty did emerge from the cab, he ran straight for the hood of Linda Wilkins's Peugeot. Wilkins spent another hour searching for the cat, but when she couldn't find him, she assumed he had run off.

A little while later, Wilkins went for a drive into town and again heard the sound of cat cries in the car: the kitten was still somewhere under the hood of her Peugeot! After another hour of searching, Wilkins became desperate. Afraid that she had injured the kitten during the drive into town, she decided that it was better to get him out immediately rather than wait for him to come out on his own—if he still could. So she called a mechanic, put the car on blocks, and had the engine dismantled.

The kitten, named Purr-geot by the end of his ordeal, had lodged himself in the engine's manifold and was safe and sound. The mechanic didn't charge Linda for the service, and Purr-geot got a good meal before Wilkins went in search of an adoptive family for him. Her comments on the incident: "He obviously loves the warmth of car engines."

Meow-valous Molly

In April 2006, a calamity of pet proportions snarled traffic (foot and vehicle) in lower Manhattan. Molly the Mouser, an 11-month-old black cat who lived at Myers of Keswick, a deli on Hudson Street, was meowing pitifully inside the building's walls. New York City police and firefighters rushed to the scene and kept an ear out for the kitty until Mike Pastore and members of the city's Animal Care and Control department arrived. What followed were 14 tense days during which Pastore and his team used drills, miniature cameras, and raw fish to try to locate and draw out

Molly. There were moments when the men thought they'd failed: For several days, Molly was quiet and rescuers feared she'd died. But when her meowing began again, they forged ahead with renewed zeal.

Finally, on April 14, a rescuer found Molly wedged into a crawl space between bricks and a piece of sheet metal. The man pulled the cat to safety, and cheers erupted on the street outside. Peter Myers, owner of the deli, said he wasn't sure how Molly ended up inside the building's walls—perhaps she slipped through a crack while exploring—but no matter. Myers was just glad to have Molly safe. For her first meal, he offered her bits of roasted pork and some sardines, and then he sent her home with his daughter to recuperate. Despite being trapped for two weeks, Myers said Molly was "in great shape," and she went back to her mousing duties soon after.

* * *

Trapped cat rescues are nothing new in New York City. In fact, as far back as 1927, New Yorkers were stopping in their tracks to save cats. That year, a tabby named Romeo got stuck in a revolving door at police headquarters. While volunteers struggled to free him, business in the building came to a standstill, and all visitors to the station had to come and go through the back door.

Organizing for the Ocelot

The endangered southwestern ocelot
gets help from an unlikely source.

At the very tip of Texas lives a type of wild cat called
the southwestern ocelot. About twice the length of a
regular house cat, the ocelot's fur is tawny and covered
with dark spots; its tail is ringed like a raccoon's. Ocelots
are nocturnal hunters who spend their days resting in
trees. They eat small animals like rodents, fish, and birds,
and unlike most cats, they love to swim.

But over the last 50 years, hunting, poaching, and habitat loss have threatened America's ocelot population.
Thousands of these cats once roamed a large range that
included the southern United States (Texas, Louisiana,
Arkansas, New Mexico, and Arizona) and Central and
South America. But today, they're crowded into a small
area along the Texas-Mexico border, and scientists esti-
mate that only 80 to 100 ocelots are left in the wild. For
this reason, ocelots have been on the endangered species
list since 1972.

Ranchers to the Rescue
For some Texas ranchers, this is unacceptable.

Stereotypically the enemies of wildlife (because they need to clear so much land for farming), ranchers are slowly coming around to the plight of the ocelot. Two ranchers in particular have become heroes to these wild cats.

Michael Corbett owns a 4,500-acre ranch in south Texas that's home to a small group of ocelots. Farming and cattle raising have become too costly, Corbett says, so instead of clearing his land and displacing the wild animals that live there, Corbett allows hunting on his property (only of legal game like doves, ducks, and deer) and has enrolled his ranch in the U.S. Fish and Wildlife Service's (FWS) Conservation Reserve Program. This government-sponsored incentive program pays rent to ranchers who set aside private land as habitat for wild animals. The ranchers continue to own the land, but the wildlife on it is protected as if on a federal reserve.

Frank Yturria is another Texas rancher who has made protecting the ocelots a priority. He has also allowed the U.S. government (by way of the FWS) to section off 600 acres of his 15,000-acre ranch for use as an ocelot habitat. Yturria is also on staff at the FWS and tries to recruit other ranchers to participate in programs like these.

Some people might wonder why a rancher would do so much to protect a predatory animal. But Yturria grew up in the area during the 1930s

and 1940s, when ocelots and other big cats roamed the Texas countryside, and he explains his mission by saying he hopes to preserve some of the lifestyle he remembers as a child.

On the Loose

In November 2005, an ocelot escaped from the Bergen County Zoo in New Jersey. The animal had been held in the zoo's administration building/hospital while her outdoor exhibit was being renovated. On the morning of November 26, zookeepers discovered that the ocelot's cage had been opened, and the animal was gone. A statewide search followed, and even though residents near the zoo feared the wild cat on the loose, zookeepers assured them that she posed no threat to people. On December 13, the ocelot's life on the lam came to an end. She got caught in a cage near the administration building from which she'd fled. Zookeepers took her back to her exhibit, but how she escaped from the locked administration building and where she spent her two weeks on the run remain a mystery.

* * *

More than 20 species of wild cats—including Mexican bobcats, snow leopards, Florida panthers, and mountain lions—are included on the U.S. Fish and Wildlife Service's threatened and endangered species list.

Scaredy-Cat!

Cats get a bad rap when it comes to luck—what with black cats being linked to witches and all. But you might be surprised to learn that, according to some superstitions, cats are actually the bearers of good fortune.

A cat in a newborn's crib will keep evil spirits at bay.

—*Russia*

A shopkeeper who keeps cats in his stores will have good luck: the older and more ugly the cats, the luckier they are.

—*China*

Burying a black cat in your field on Christmas Eve ensures a good harvest.

—*Transylvania and Poland*

A fisherman's wife who keeps black cats will ensure her husband's return.

—*England*

Having a cat in the theater is good luck, especially if it goes to the bathroom backstage.

—*The United States*

Cat Questions—Answered

Cats do the darndest things. Here are answers
to some common cat-behavior questions.

Why do cats always land on their feet?

Cats don't always land on their feet, but they've got a natural reflex that allows them to right themselves more easily than other animals during a fall. This reflex is complex, but basically, senses in their inner ears give cats quick information about where the ground is in relation to their heads. They then can quickly flip their bodies right-side up and use their tails for balance. Cats need about 1.8 seconds to right themselves during a fall. This means that when a cat falls a short distance he's less likely to land on his feet than a cat who falls a long way.

Why do people think cats have nine lives?

The idea that cats have nine lives is a superstition that evolved from people's experiences with cats surviving high falls. The cat's "righting" reflex helps a great deal, of course, but cats have other natural defenses that help them. Because cats land on four feet instead of two, for example, they don't hit the ground with as much force as two-footed animals (ahem . . . humans) do. Also, when cats fall from a high elevation, they spread their legs out so that their bodies create an umbrella shape. This allows their bodies to act as parachutes, lessening the speed with which they fall and making the landing softer.

Why do cats knead?

When kittens are nursing, they knead against their mothers' bellies to draw out milk. A relaxed adult cat kneads your leg or a couch cushion to show that he's happy and content, as he was when he was a nursing baby.

Why do cats see well in the dark?

Cats can't see in total darkness any better than we can, but in semidarkness, their sight is fairly good. Because cats evolved as nocturnal hunters, their eyes had to pick up very slight bits of moon or starlight to help find their prey.

How well do cats hear?

They hear much better than we do, but when it comes to ranges of sound, not as well as dogs. However, cats hear high-pitched sounds better than humans or dogs, a skill that comes from eons of skulking through the bushes listening for movement that might indicate a meal.

Why doesn't my cat like to eat refrigerated food?

Cats of old didn't eat refrigerated foods, and your cat likely doesn't want to either. In the wild, cats eat their kills fresh, at body temperature. So instead of giving kitty refrigerated treats, try serving them at room temperature or briefly warming them in the microwave—not too hot, though; kitty doesn't want to burn her tongue either.

Why do cats hate water?

The ancestors of modern house cats were desert animals. They didn't have water around, so they didn't grow accustomed to water. But not all cats hate water. Some wild cats (tigers, for example) love to swim, and kittens who grow up being exposed to water generally don't mind it.

Why don't cats need to drink a lot of water?

Again, cats are desert animals, so their kidneys adapted to life without a lot of water. That's why their urine is so concentrated; their kidneys can expel lots of waste with very little fluid. In some cases, cats don't need to drink any water at all. Researchers have found that some cats whose diet is made up of 70 percent canned food get all the fluid they need from their diet. Never let diet substitute for water, however. Veterinarians stress that cats should always have a supply of fresh water on hand, whether they drink it regularly or not.

*   *   *

Did You Know?

One-third of cat-allergic people have at least one cat at home.

Yule Better Watch Out

Children around the world know all about the perils of landing on Santa's infamous Naughty List: behave badly enough, and you'll get a lump of coal on Christmas Day. As unwelcome a gift as that may be, it pales in comparison to what children in Iceland face during the Yuletide season.

Before Christianity took hold in Iceland in A.D. 1000, locals celebrated Yule, a festival that coincided with the winter solstice on December 21 and marked the gradual return of longer days and increasingly warmer weather. Eventually, Yule was overtaken by Christmas celebrations, but some Yuletide traditions, like the Yule Cat, continue to this day.

Dressed to Live

According to legend, Icelandic children who don't receive gifts of new clothing in time for Christmas risk being devoured by the Yule Cat, a giant, hungry feline. Jóhannes úr Kötlum, a popular 20th-century Icelandic poet and the author of *The Yule Cat Poem*, best described the creature. According to Kötlum, the cat has "glaring eyes," whiskers "sharp as bristles," and "if one heard a pitiful 'meow,' something evil would happen soon."

Luckily, children can avoid the Yule Cat simply by

wearing their new clothes—anything from a bright new Christmas sweater to a freshly knit pair of socks. While clad in these garments, children should stand proudly at their windows on Christmas Eve so the Yule Cat will see their new clothes and pass them by.

The Yule Cat story is grisly, but like many legends, it once had a purpose. Avoiding the Yule Cat gives Icelanders an added incentive to prepare the autumn wool before the Yuletide season, thereby ensuring that they will have enough warm clothing to last through the winter. The Yule Cat also teaches that industriousness is rewarded, procrastination is punished, and children must always be provided for.

Hungry Gryla

Scary as he is, the Yule Cat is no wild beast; he's a pet. According to Icelandic legend, he belongs to Gryla, a menacing ogress who lives in a dank cave with her husband, her 13 children, and the family's pet, the Yule Cat. Gryla has a long tail, hooves, and burning eyes, and she also has a dastardly habit of stealing badly behaved children and slipping them into her sack during Yule. Unfortunately, these children never have a chance to repent, as they soon end up in Gryla's oversized cauldron and, eventually, in her ravenous belly.

Gryla first appeared in print in a 13th-century manuscript entitled *Snorra-Edda,* a treatise on poetics and mythology written especially for Icelandic writers. The

Yule Cat made his print debut six centuries later. But as with most folklore, both characters likely existed in oral tradition long before their fearsome exploits were recorded officially. And Icelandic children to this day continue to try to stave off his appearance.

*　*　*

Go Cat, Go!

She feels the need, the need for speed! Motor Cat, a white-and-brown kitty from Washington, D.C., loved to ride on her owner's motorcycle. Motor used to spend a lot of time relaxing on owner J. Catman's cycle, so one day, he took her for a ride. She loved it and after about a year had become a pro. Motor had her own helmet (safety first) and especially loved to ride around the neighborhood. According to Catman, she even leaned into curves, braced herself for turns, and meowed to let him know when the light turned green.

Millions and Billions and Trillions!

Inspired by a promise to her father, author and illustrator Wanda Gág crafted a cat tale that has entertained children since it was first published in 1928.

Nurtured on the Minnesota Prairie

Wanda Hazel Gág (pronounced "gog") was born in New Ulm, Minnesota, in 1893. Her family was poor, her parents both immigrants from Germany. There were seven Gág children—Wanda was the oldest—and the family spoke only German at home. But the household was filled with art and stories. Anton Gág, Wanda's father, was a painter, photographer, and woodcarver. He supported his family by painting houses and churches, and he decorated the Gágs' own dining room ceiling with cherubs. Wanda, especially, loved to spend time with her father in his workshop. She cleaned up his tools, admired his paintings, and sometimes even painted with him.

Wanda's mother, Elisabeth, was a natural storyteller who told her children fantastic German folktales while they were growing up. She also loved photography and art and had worked in a photographer's studio as a young woman at a time when women rarely took jobs outside the home.

The Gág parents encouraged their children's creativity and imaginations. In fact, when young Wanda got in trouble at school for daydreaming, her father refused to side with her teachers. Instead, he implored her never to change.

Out of Tragedy . . .

In 1908, when Wanda was 15 years old, both Anton and Elisabeth Gág contracted tuberculosis. They grew weaker over several months, and one day, Anton pulled his eldest daughter to him, whispering, "What your papa could not do, Wanda will have to finish." He died soon after, and Wanda knew it was up to her to carry on her family's artistic legacy.

With her mother still sick and six younger children still at home, Wanda took on the responsibility of raising her family. She also continued going to school and fought attempts by relatives and social welfare agents to separate the children.

Throughout these years, she remained committed to art and literature. She drew and wrote for local publications. She also kept a diary. When she was 17, Wanda wrote, "My own motto: draw to live and live to draw." It would serve her well.

Upward and Onward

In 1914, after two of her sisters had graduated from high school, Gág moved to Saint Paul and then Minneapolis.

She attended both the St. Paul Institute of Art and the Minneapolis School of Art. There she worked on her first children's book: she provided illustrations for *A Child's Book of Folk-Lore* in 1917. She also discovered feminism after spending time with male students who didn't appreciate her artistic skills simply because she was a woman. She wrote, "I shall not rest until men are willing, and glad, to regard me as important as they." It was a cause to which she remained dedicated for the rest of her life.

After three years, Gág moved to New York City. She continued her art studies there and also got a job as an illustrator. She drew for magazine advertisements and made a good salary, but it wasn't what she really wanted to do. She wanted to write and illustrate her own stories, so she kept a journal of ideas and worked on manuscripts.

Gág shopped her manuscripts around to publishers in New York and Minneapolis, but no one was interested, so into her rejection pile they went. One of those was titled *Millions of Cats*. It was a moral tale about excess and vanity. An elderly man goes in search of a kitten for his wife but comes home with "millions and billions and trillions" of cats. The couple can't care for them all and decides to keep only the prettiest one. But who decides which is the prettiest? Eventually, all but one of the cats fight to the death, hoping to claim the title. The surviving kitty, lacking in arrogance and vanity, ultimately wins the prize.

Sweet Success

Those early publishers may not have been interested in Gág's book, but in 1926, a young children's book editor named Ernestine Evans was. The two met at an art exhibit, and Evans was impressed with Gág's drawings. When Evans asked Gág if she'd ever thought of writing a children's book, Gág pulled *Millions of Cats* out of the rejection pile and gave it to her.

Evans loved the story, its simple rhythm and rhyme, and its illustrations. She took the book back to her bosses at Coward-McCann, and they decided to publish the story. *Millions of Cats* was first printed in 1928 and was an immediate success. The format and style were a little different from what was available at the time. The book was wider than most books (10 inches wide by 7 inches high); Gág thought this gave the reader a feel for the long sweeping journey the man took to find the cats. And the illustrations used both sides of a page spread without constraint; *Millions of Cats* was the first book to employ this technique. Previously, illustrations were confined to their own pages, but Gág preferred to have the drawings flow freely across both pages.

In the years since it was first published, Wanda Gág's *Millions of Cats* has stayed in print. It also won a Newbery Medal in 1929 and paved the way for Gág's career as a children's book author and illustrator. In her lifetime, Gág wrote or illustrated (or both) more than 10 books for children. She died in June 1946.

Get These Cats
out of the Bag

Cats have found their way into many common expressions.
We've tracked down etymologies for some of them.

Playing Cat and Mouse

Suffragettes in 1913 England inspired this phrase. People who were arrested for protesting the lack of women's rights often went on hunger strikes while they were in jail. But a British law called the Prisoners' Temporary Discharge for Ill-Health Act said that inmates who were in poor health (from sickness, fasting, or any other source) should be released until they were strong enough to be incarcerated; once they'd recovered, they could be re-arrested. So hunger-striking suffragettes were repeatedly released and re-imprisoned. Critics of the government's policies on women's rights likened the British authorities to a cruel cat playing with a mouse's freedom. The critics went so far as to call the law the Cat and Mouse Act in a show of disrespect for the government's approach to suffrage.

Grinning Like a Cheshire Cat

Most people think this phrase comes from Lewis Carroll's *Alice in Wonderland* and that it refers to the mischievous Cheshire cat character in the book. Actually, though, the phrase predates Carroll, and the author likely borrowed it himself. There are two proposed origins for this phrase. One comes from a type of cheese (called Cheshire cheese) sold in Carroll's day and molded to look like a grinning cat's face. Another explanation is that the phrase was originally "to grin like a Cheshire Caterling," in reference to a 16th-century British swordsman named Caterling who was known for his menacing grin. Over time, Caterling was shortened to Cat.

Letting the Cat out of the Bag

There are two possible origins of this phrase. The first comes from medieval Europe, when merchants at markets sold piglets in small paper sacks. Sometimes the merchants tried to trick customers by selling them kittens instead of piglets (a ruse the customer didn't discover until he had paid and left with the wiggling sack). As more and more people got wise to the trick, they demanded that merchants selling piglets open the bags before a customer paid. When someone caught a trickster trying to sell a kitten, the secret was out. This practice also was the origin of the phrase "never buy a pig in a poke," because the paper sacks containing the piglets or kittens were called "pokes."

A second possibility is that the phrase originated with the cat-o'-nine-tails, which was stored on British sailing ships in a baize bag. When it came time to punish a sailor with the "cat," the whip had to be pulled out of the bag, thus revealing to the sailor the punishment that awaited him.

There's More Than One Way to Skin a Cat

The origin of this phrase, meaning that there's more than one way to do something, actually has no connection to cats at all. The complete expression is "there's more than one way to skin a catfish," and the saying derives from fishermen trying to remove a catfish's tough skin from its delicate meat. Many fishermen used trial and error to find the best way to skin a catfish while keeping the fillets intact.

It's Raining Cats and Dogs

The first printed use of this phrase was in Jonathan Swift's 1738 *A Complete Collection of Polite and Ingenious Conversation*. But the phrase has at least two possible origins. The first comes from Norse mythology, where cats represented rain, and dogs, wind. Heavy downpours were said to be "cats and dogs." A second explanation has its roots in the poor drainage systems in medieval European cities. When it rained, city streets often flooded and drowned stray cats and dogs. When the city's residents took to the streets to assess damage caused by the storms, they saw the animals and equated heavy rain with them.

There's Not Enough Room to Swing a Cat

This phrase has its roots in a type of punishment doled out on 18th- and 19th-century British sailing ships. Sailors found guilty of various infractions were often punished with a leather whip called the cat-o'-nine-tails. The whip was called a cat because it left welts on a sailor's back that resembled large cat scratches, and its nine tails referred to the nine braided thongs (or tails) coming off the whip's handle. Most of the whippings took place on the ship's deck, where there was enough room to swing the whip fully and where the rest of the crew would be sure to see the example made of the offending sailor. Punishing the sailor below deck was out of the question because there wasn't enough room down there to swing the "cat."

Cat Got Your Tongue?

No one knows for sure how this phrase got started, but there are a couple of theories. One is that sailors who were whipped with the cat-o'-nine-tails were rendered speechless from pain. Another posits that the expression comes from a Middle Eastern tradition whereby soldiers punished a liar by cutting out his tongue and feeding it to cats. Either way, the expression became popular during the late 1800s and first appeared in print around 1911. Initially, it specifically referred to children who refused to answer their parents' direct questions. But over time, the expression evolved to a more general question for anyone who was shy or didn't speak forthrightly.

How Do I Love Thee?

*People who say cats aren't as affectionate as dogs just
don't understand how felines communicate. Here are
seven ways your cat lets you know she loves you.*

1. She licks you. This means she's grooming you and
showing affection. It's like a kiss.

2. She brings you a dead mouse or bird. Humans
might be horrified at such an offering, but to a cat, there's
no better present.

3. She likes to rest in your lap. Cats like warm
places, and laps are one of the best. But a
cat will only willingly climb into the
lap of someone she knows and
trusts.

**4. She sucks on or
licks your clothes.**
Ewww! For you maybe, but for
your cat, this is a way to get to know you better. Cats have
a scent organ on the roof of their mouth, so licking things
allows them to gather lots of information about a person.

5. She puts a paw on your arm. This is a gesture of contentment, a way your cat says she's happy to be with you.

6. She wraps her tail around your legs. Your cat is territorial, and wrapping her tail around you shows she's claiming you as her own.

7. She holds her tail upright. When cats don't like someone (whether a person or another animal), they approach cautiously, with their tails down. If your kitty approaches you with her tail straight up, it means she trusts you.

* * *

Ted's Adventure

In 1994, Californian Chris Inglis's black cat Ted jumped out of a car window and disappeared. Ten years later, thanks to a microchip in Ted's skin, feline and human were reunited. Folks at the Peninsula Humane Society near San Francisco, where Ted had been found, tracked Inglis down using the information on the microchip.

When man and cat were reunited, it was just like old times. Ted rubbed his face against Inglis's hand and seemed thrilled to be back with his owner. Inglis said that one of Ted's favorite things to do was go for rides in the car, his front paws resting on the dashboard, so the friends went for a drive . . . this time, with the windows closed.

Felines in Folsom

Stray cats on exhibit at the zoo? Here's how.

When Robert Bauder's garage door broke several decades ago, a couple of feral cats in search of a safe haven sneaked into the garage and soon moved into the attic through crawl spaces in the walls. Over time, they multiplied and settled into the attic, garage, shed, dog run, chicken coop, and even a camp trailer on Bauder's four-acre Citrus Heights, California, property.

Here, Kitty Kitty

It might have been easy to seal the holes, lock the garage, and evict the cats, but Bauder got attached to the colony.

He named the cats, provided food for them, and buried them when they died. Bauder even went so far as to knock holes in most of the rooms in his home so the cats could roam freely. None of the kitties

ever became tame enough for him to hold, but some would allow a pat every now and then.

In 2002, Bauder was diagnosed with terminal cancer, and he knew he had to do something to provide for his cats after his death. So he called a local animal rescue organization called Folsom Feline Rescue and met up with volunteer Lisa James. James was touched by Bauder's affection for the animals, and she vowed to help find the cats a home. First, she and Bauder rounded up the many kittens on the property and put them up for adoption. Then James contacted the Folsom City Sanctuary Zoo, hoping the remaining adult cats (12 in all) could move in there. The sanctuary, located in northern California, houses wild animals in need of tender loving care. Some were wild animals kept as pets but later discarded. Others were injured and left to die in the wild. And most are native to North America. It was an ideal site for the cats.

Folsom to the Rescue

Bauder died in 2005 at the age of 84. Days later, the sanctuary announced plans to exhibit Bauder's beloved feral cat colony. Earlier that year, the sanctuary had exhibited adoptable cats from a local animal shelter. That exhibit was temporary but popular. Zoo officials hoped that the new feral-cat exhibit would draw crowds as well. They also wanted to use Bauder's exhibit to educate people about the importance of spay and neuter programs to minimize unwanted cat populations. Bauder's heirs donated $15,000 to get the exhibit started, and the zoo raised another $5,000.

The adult cats from Bauder's property are now housed at the Folsom City Sanctuary Zoo. The feral cat exhibit opened to the public in the summer of 2006.

*   *   *

Getting Their Just Deserts

A pair of Florida kitty-nappers received sentences of 150 hours of community service for snatching Mr. Kibbles, a black cat from Fort Lauderdale, and abandoning him 15 miles away in the Everglades. Apparently, Mr. Kibbles had used the kitty-nappers' truck for a litter box, but a judge didn't think that was a good enough reason to pilfer the cat. Mr. Kibbles managed to survive the ordeal and found his way home again, where he was welcomed with open arms by his owner, 12-year-old Maggie Leonard. Maggie was pleased with the judge's decision. "That's what they get for taking an innocent cat," she said.

Attack Cat?

Is Lewis really dangerous, or is he just misunderstood?

Fairfield, Connecticut, is a town of about 58,000 people on Long Island Sound; a town where lawns are well-kept, kids ride their bikes on safe sidewalks, and cats prowl their neighbors' yards. But for one cat, dubbed the "terrorist of Sunset Circle," there will be no prowling. Lewis will spend the rest of his life under house arrest because, according to his neighbors, he's got a wicked side.

Lewis Lunges

At first glance, he's unassuming—a black-and-white kitty with a black-spotted nose and long hair. Lewis is a typical cat, says his owner Ruth Cisero: he likes climbing trees, skulking in corners, chasing birds. And he loves to be outside. But in March 2006, Lewis found himself in trouble with the law. One of his neighbors, Janet Kettman, claimed Lewis attacked her as she headed for her front door. "I never saw it coming," Kettman said. "He attacked me from the back. I had eight big gouges and three bites." Those injuries landed Kettman in the hospital and Lewis in a heap of trouble.

Kettman wasn't Lewis's first or last victim. Rumor has it that he's attacked as many as six people, but we know of only two others: an Avon lady and a neighbor. When that neighbor complained, animal control officers got involved. They arrested Cisero and contacted the district attorney, who charged Cisero with reckless endangerment.

Say It Ain't So!

The first judge who heard the case offered Cisero probation if Lewis were euthanized, and prosecutors said they'd drop the charges if the cat were declawed. But Cisero refused. She didn't think the kitty deserved a death sentence or to lose his claws for his crimes, and she wasn't entirely sure he hadn't been acting in self-defense. Once, she said, Lewis came home covered in raw eggs, and another time, he was soaked, as though someone had turned a hose on him. Furthermore, said Cisero, in the five years since she'd adopted Lewis, he had never attacked her or anyone in her home. So rather than take the deal, Cisero got her own lawyer and decided to fight it out in court.

Lewis Goes to Court

In June 2006, the case went to trial, and due to all the attention Lewis was getting (even CNN profiled his story), the courtroom was packed. Animal lovers and animal rights activists traveled far and wide to show their support. Russ Mead from the Best Friends Animal Society, an animal sanctuary in Kanab, Utah, was there. Mead planned to file for custody of Lewis if the judge deemed the kitty too dangerous to remain in Connecticut. Rosemarie Gravis came all the way from Florida to show her support after reading a magazine article about Lewis. She said, "Ruth should not be separated from that cat, because we are bonded to our animals."

Presiding judge Patrick Carroll III heard the evidence of possible self-defense and listened to neighbors' claims that Lewis was more sinister than regular cats. In the end, Judge Carroll decided to spare Lewis's life. He sentenced Lewis to a lifetime of house arrest, put Cisero on probation for two years, and ordered that she complete 50 hours of community service. It was a resolution Cisero (and Lewis) could live with. She said, "We'll do our best to make him happy . . . like everybody in life, you make adjustments."

* * *

The Long Fall

In the 1970s, Andy, a cat who belonged to Florida senator Ken Myer, fell from a 16th-floor apartment window. Andy plunged a record 200 feet and survived.

Ah-Choo!

Are you allergic to your cat, or is your cat allergic to you?

Cats have long been considered an asthmatic's night-mare. The American Academy of Allergy, Asthma and Immunology estimates that 15 million people are allergic to felines. But these days, veterinarians are seeing more and more cats who suffer from allergies themselves.

Around the House
Approximately 1 cat in 200 has feline asthma. As in humans, asthma symptoms include coughing, wheezing, and shortness of breath. Feline asthma isn't new. In fact, the first references to it showed up in scientific journals during the early 20th century. But veterinarians do notice that more cats seem to be coming down with the disease than ever before.

They suspect it's because conscientious cat owners are keeping their kitties indoors exclusively. Vets agree that an indoor life is safer for your cat than an outdoor one. Cats who stay in the house don't have to cope with dangers like cars, bad weather, and other animals, so they have a longer lifespan (15 years on average for an indoor cat versus 11 years for cats in general). But they're also exposed for longer periods to potential allergens like cigarette smoke, household dust, and even human dandruff. These things can irritate a cat's skin and lungs and cause reactions ranging from rashes to full-blown asthma.

A Bath Does a Body Good

The best way to deal with allergies is to remove the source of the irritation, say veterinarians. So making sure your home is free of triggers like dust and smoke can go a long way in helping your cat feel better. Experts also recommend the following:

- Wash your cat's bedding (and your own) in hot water at least twice a month. This will kill dust mites, the primary culprits in dust allergies.
- Don't smoke inside.
- Give your cat a bath. It's no secret that cats are averse to water, but a bath with an oatmeal-based or otherwise hypoallergenic shampoo will probably soothe your cat's skin irritation. A bath about once a month should be often enough for you and your cat to notice a difference.
- Your cat may actually have a food allergy. Believe it or not, food allergies in cats can trigger asthma-like symptoms, and there are cat food companies that offer specially formulated diets for cats with food allergies.
- Consult a vet for advice. There are many medical options available to people whose cats have severe allergies, and although feline asthma is usually a mild condition, severe cases can require medical attention.

For the Cat Who Has Everything

We browsed the Internet and tracked down some outrageous cat accessories. Take a look at our favorites.

1. Thing in a Bag

The classic paper bag has been given a 21st-century twist. "Thing in a Bag" is a battery-powered . . . well . . . bag that wiggles, rustles, and crinkles to your kitty's heart's content. More traditional versions of the paper bag (the kind that come from the store) are subject to wear and tear, but the Thing in a Bag features a rip-resistant finish to protect it from sharp claws.

2. Jewels

For fashionable felines, a simple cloth collar just won't do, so it's lucky that a wide variety of collars and jewelry is available to suit any special occasion. Owners can choose from a collar with their pet's name spelled out in rhinestone studs or a necklace made with real crystals. And for those truly special occasions, tiny tiaras let everyone know who really owns the place.

3. DVDs

If your cat's not enough of a couch potato, keep him
entertained with "cat TV." These DVDs (and VHS) feature fish, birds, even the occasional squirrel or guinea pig,
and include natural sounds for hours of enjoyment with no
need for channel surfing.

4. Spa Treatments

After a long day of catnapping, eating, and napping
again, your kitty can relax with the Cat Spa. This
beauty kit includes a massager, gum-stimulating chew-
able parts, and self-grooming tools for the ultimate experience in feline relaxation. To take the spa experience
one step further, some pet-grooming salons now feature
exclusive cat services (dogs aren't even allowed on the
premises!). Complete packages feature nail trimming,
ear cleaning, haircuts and shampoos, a spritz of cologne,
and a complimentary bow. Throw in some catnip aroma-
therapy for a truly chic spa day.

5. The Treat Machine

Kitty found the litter box? Great! She didn't scratch the
sofa? Even better! Reward her with the Kitty Food and
Treat Machine. Built to resemble a gumball machine, this
device dispenses treats at the press of a paw-shaped lever.
No need for opposable thumbs here.

6. The Fun Run

Whether your pet is a mountain-lion-in-training or a city pet, she'll always be able to play in style. The Fun Run, an enclosed mesh tube for outdoor play, offers the sights and smells of the great outdoors without the temptation of scrambling over the fence.

7. A Futon

A patch of sunlight might be Fluffy's favorite sleeping spot, but what is she to do when the sun goes down? A cat-sized futon is perfect for nighttime naps and has extra room for sleepovers with friends so that she won't commit the "faux paw" of relegating her animal guests to the floor.

8. A Radio-Controlled Spider

Sharpen your pet's hunting skills with a radio-controlled spider. This new take on the toy mouse can even reverse and change direction. You just keep control of the remote and watch as your cat chases the spider around the room.

* * *

"There are two means of refuge from the miseries of life: music and cats."
—*Albert Schweitzer, musician and philosopher*

Seuss Writes
The Cat in the Hat

*One of the first felines kids get to know is Seuss's
"Cat in the Hat." Here we wax poetic about the good
doctor and the cat who taught children to read.*

The Doctor Is In

Dr. Seuss was born Theodor Seuss Geisel in Springfield,
Massachusetts, on March 2, 1904. He attended Dartmouth
College in New Hampshire and began his writing career as
an editor for the *Jack-O-Lantern*, the school's literary magazine. But after he and some friends threw a drinking party,
college administrators forced him to resign as the *Jack-O-
Lantern's* editor—this was during Prohibition—and to promise that he would no longer write for the publication. Rather
than forsake his affiliation with the magazine, Geisel began
writing under a pseudonym: Seuss ("Dr." came later).

After graduation, Geisel went to work as a cartoonist.
Magazines including the *Saturday Evening Post*, *Vanity Fair*,
and *Judge* ran his work. In 1937, he sold his first book: *And
to Think That I Saw It On Mulberry Street*, which he wrote
and illustrated himself. Twenty-seven publishers turned
down *Mulberry Street* before New York's Vanguard Press
decided to buy it.

Fun with Phonics

Dr. Seuss quickly earned a reputation as a children's author and illustrator, and a unique one at that. His wacky, vividly illustrated stories appeared during an era when dull Dick and Jane books were used to teach children to read because they used only a few easy words and repeated them for effect. New readers then memorized those words so they could recognize them in other books. But Dr. Seuss wanted to write books that both educated and entertained, and he believed phonics (the study of sounds), rather than rote memorization, was the best way to teach reading.

In the late 1950s, Vanguard Press approached him with an idea: write and illustrate a Seussian story using only the words new readers can recognize. Seuss chose 220 of those words—*cat* was one of them—and the result was *The Cat in the Hat*. His final draft was 1,702 words long. Fifty-four of the "new reader" words appear once, 33 appear twice, and the most common words (like *I*, *the*, and *not*) show up approximately 30 times each.

To Press

The book arrived in stores in March 1957, and almost immediately, it caught on with kids. In its first month, *The Cat in the Hat* sold 12,000 copies. That trend continued for several years afterward. By 1960, more than 1 million copies had been sold.

The book's success also inspired Random House (the

owner of Vanguard Press) to start a division specifically for new readers called Beginner Books. Dr. Seuss was one of the people in charge of Beginner Books. He wrote other stories for the imprint (*Green Eggs and Ham,* among them) and mentored writers who submitted ideas and were charged with the task of using only words on the "new reader" list.

The Cat in the Hat revolutionized education in America. Schools used the book and others like it to teach children to read using rhymes and phonics, rather than rote memorization. The book's popularity also proved that colorful illustrations and silly tales were more enticing to young readers than more traditional texts.

Today, Seuss's story of two youngsters left home alone by their mother and visited by a mysterious (and naughty) feline is the ninth best-selling children's hardcover book in the United States.

Dr. Seuss published 44 books in his lifetime. He died on September 24, 1991.

Thufferin' Thuccotash!

*It was a match made in Hollywood. This is how a bumbling
cartoon cat and his wide-eyed nemesis became a pair for the ages.*

First Came Tweety . . .

Created by: Looney Tunes director Bob Clampett

Inspiration: "In school I remember seeing nature films
which showed newborn birds in a nest," Clampett
recalled. "They always looked funny to me. One time I
kicked around the idea of twin baby birds called 'Twick 'n'
Tweet' who were precursors of Tweety."

Later, Tweety's basic design and "innocent stare at the
camera" were copied from an even more unusual source: a
nude baby picture of Clampett himself. That's probably
why the original Tweety was pink.

Debut: *Tale of Two Kitties*, a 1942 spoof of Abbott and
Costello (who appeared as bumbling cats named Babbit and
Cat-stello). The little nameless bird's opening line, "I tawt I
taw a puddy tat!" made the cartoon—and the character—a
hit. Mel Blanc (who also did Daffy Duck, Bugs Bunny,
Porky Pig, etc.) supplied the voice. He recorded it at normal
speed, but directors played it back at a higher speed.

Tweety's next cartoon, *Birdy and the Beast* (1944), gave
him a name and personality. But in 1946, movie censors

decided the pink bird "looked naked" and insisted Clampett put a pair of pants on him. The cartoonist refused. Instead, he gave Tweety "yellow feathers and a slimmer body."

Then Came Sylvester . . .

Created by: Oscar-winning Looney Tunes director Friz Freleng

Inspiration: Freleng designed the cat "to look subtly like a clown. I gave him a big, red nose and a very low crotch, which was supposed to look like he was wearing baggy pants."

According to Mel Blanc, the unwitting model was Looney Tunes's "jowly executive producer Johnny Burton."

Debut: A 1945 cartoon, *Life with Feathers*

The plot: "A love bird has a major fight with his wife and decides to end it all by letting a cat (Sylvester, before he had a name) eat him." The cat's first words on finding a bird who wants to be eaten: "Thufferin' thuccotash!" Sylvester's voice—also supplied by Mel Blanc—sounded more like Blanc's real speaking voice than any of his other characters. It was actually the same voice he used for Daffy Duck, but not sped up. Says Blanc in his autobiography, *That's Not All Folks:*

> Sylvester has always been a favorite of mine. He's always been the easiest character for me to play. When I was first shown the model sheet of Sylvester, with his floppy jowls and generally disheveled appearance, I

said to Friz Freleng, 'A big sloppy cat should have a big shthloppy voice! He should spray even more than Daffy.' While recording Sylvester cartoons, my scripts would get so covered with saliva that I'd repeatedly have to wipe them clean.

Sylvester's first cartoon was nominated for an Oscar, and he appeared (still nameless) in two more before Clampett got permission to team him with Tweety in 1947. However, Clampett left Warner Brothers just as he began working on the project.

Together at Last

Freleng took over the cartoon. He gave the cat a name—Thomas (changed to Sylvester in 1948 by animator Tedd Pierce, who thought a slobbering cat needed a name that could be slobbered)—and made Tweety a little friendlier. "I made him look more like a charming baby, with a bigger head and blue eyes," Freleng explained.

In their first cartoon together, *Tweety Pie*, Thomas catches Tweety, who's freezing in the winter cold. But before he can eat the bird, Thomas's owner saves Tweety and brings him home. Tweety then proceeds to terrorize the cat and take over the house.

Tweety Pie earned the Warner Brothers cartoon studio its first Academy Award, and the pair made 55 more cartoons together.

Find the Fictional Feline!

*There are 34 fictional cats in the puzzle
on the following page. Can you find them all?*

CATBERT	MOG
CHESHIRE CAT	MORRIS
COWARDLY LION	MR BIGGLESWORTH
CROOKSHANKS	OLD DEUTERONOMY
DUCHESS	PUSS IN BOOTS
ELSA	RITA
FELIX	RUM TUM TUGGER
FRITZ	SHERE KHAN
GARFIELD	STIMPY
HEATHCLIFF	THAT DARN CAT
HELLO KITTY	THE CAT IN THE HAT
HOBBES	THREE LITTLE KITTENS
KOKO	TIGGER
KRAZY KAT	TOM
LEO	TOONCES
MEHITABEL	TOP CAT
MEW	YUM-YUM

*For the answers, and to learn more about
these cats, turn to page 224.*

219

Answers

TV Tabbies, p. 10

1. B	2. A	3. G	4. H
5. D	6. E	7. C	8. F

Cats in Song, p. 48

1. D. Born in South Wales, Tom Jones became a star in the United States in 1965 with the release of the song "It's Not Unusual." "What's New Pussycat" followed that same year.

2. A. The Stray Cats' 1981 debut album included two Top-10 hits: "Rock This Town" and "Stray Cat Strut."

3. I. For the 2005 album *Songs of the Cat*, humorist Garrison Keillor and German opera singer Frederica von Stade teamed up to pay homage to their feline friends. "My Grandmother's Cat" is one of 20 kitty-themed songs on the album.

4. F. A 15-piece swing band à la the Brian Setzer Orchestra, the Cat Pack hails from the United Kingdom.

5. G. Janet Jackson included this song on her 1989 *Rhythm Nation 1814* album. "Black Cat" is one of the only rock-style songs the singer has recorded during her career.

6. H. The blues-rock-country group Little Feat formed in Los Angeles in 1970 and over the next few years released several albums, including *Sailin' Shoes*, *Feats Don't Fail Me Now*, and *Dixie Chicken*, which inspired Martie and Emily Erwin (bluegrass-playing sisters from Dallas, Texas) to form a band called the Dixie Chicks.

7. B. Harry Chapin's "Cat's in the Cradle" has been covered in several different musical styles, including a hard-rock version by Ugly Kid Joe (in 1992), a country version by Ricky Skaggs (1995), and a rap sample duet by Sarah McLachlan and Darryl McDaniels of Run-DMC fame (2006).

8. C. Phoebe Buffay (played by Lisa Kudrow) first sang "Smelly Cat," her signature tune, during the 1995 *Friends* episode entitled "The One with the Baby on the Bus."

9. E. Peggy Lee cowrote and recorded this song in 1955 for the Walt Disney film *Lady and the Tramp*.

First Felines, p. 86

1. F   2. G   3. C   4. A
5. D   6. E   7. B

Kit Lit, p. 129

1. A. Laura Ingalls Wilder published her first Little House book in 1932. Over the next 11 years, she wrote 7 more in the series (three others were published posthumously).

2. C. Because the "Three Little Kittens" (like most nursery rhymes) was authored anonymously, no one knows for sure how long it's been around. We do know, though, that in 1858, R. N. Ballantyne was the first person to publish the poem as part of his illustrated children's book, *Good Little Pig's Library*.

3. C. One of the best-known writers of animal stories for children, Marguerite Henry grew up in a house without any pets.

4. B. Lewis Carroll's real name was Charles Lutwidge Dodgson, and in addition to being a writer, he was also a photographer, mathematician, logician, and clergyman.

5. B. Pronouncing Hermione's name was a challenge for Harry Potter readers. J. K. Rowling says she tried to help them out by inserting a phonetic spelling into the fourth book ("Her-my-o-nee") but also admitted that she enjoyed some of the mispronunciations; her favorite was "Hermy-one."

6. A. Aslan is the Turkish word for "lion." Many Persian and Ottoman kings took aslan as a title, so it's fitting that C. S. Lewis chose this name for Narnia's true ruler.

7. B. Writer Edward Lear came from a big family. He had 19 older brothers and sisters.

8. C. Many of Beatrix Potter's characters first appeared in letters she wrote to friends. The letters made their way to publishers who so enjoyed the stories that they decided to turn them into books. Peter Rabbit and

Squirrel Nutkin are two of the most famous characters who made the leap from personal letters to published works.

9. C. "Erin Hunter" is actually a pseudonym for two British authors (Cherith Baldry and Kate Cary) who write the Warriors series.

10. B. Louisa May Alcott most identified with Jo March, the outspoken, tomboyish, second-oldest March sister. In very "Jo-like" fashion, Alcott once said of her childhood, "No boy could be my friend till I had beaten him in a race, and no girl if she refused to climb trees, leap fences."

Find the Fictional Feline!, p. 218

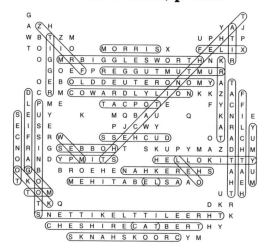

Want to know more about the cats in the word search puzzle? Even the most devoted cat lover may not know all of them. Here's a cat-alog of who they are and where they come from.

Catbert
"Evil director of human resources" in the *Dilbert* comic strip

Cheshire Cat
He vanishes, leaving only a grin, in *Alice in Wonderland*

Cowardly Lion
One of Dorothy's pals in *The Wizard of Oz*

Crookshanks
Hermione's pet cat in the *Harry Potter* books

Duchess
One of Disney's Aristocats, voiced by Eva Gabor

Elsa
Lioness in 1966's *Born Free*

Felix
Black-and-white cat of
silent films

Fritz
Cat of "underground"
comics, by Robert Crumb

Garfield
Jim Davis's widely syndi-
cated comic strip cat

Heathcliff
George Gately's fun-loving
orange comic cat

Hello Kitty
Popular Japanese cartoon
cat who usually wears a
bow over her left ear

Hobbes
Calvin's stuffed tiger in the
Calvin and Hobbes comic
strip

Koko
Brilliant Siamese cat in

Lilian Jackson Braun's
best-selling mysteries

Krazy Kat
Cat of George Herman
comics (1913–1944)

Leo
Star of MGM's lion logo

Mehitabel
Archy's pal in Don
Marquis's Archy and
Mehitabel books

Mew
Feline Pokémon character

Mog
Cat hero of Judith Kerr's
children's books

Morris
9Lives cat food mascot in
TV commercials; the
"world's most finicky cat"

Mr. Bigglesworth
Dr. Evil's cat in the Austin
Powers movies

Old Deuteronomy
Wise old patriarch in *Cats*, the Broadway play based on T. S. Eliot's *Old Possum's Book of Practical Cats*

Puss in Boots
Cat in an old fairy tale, and a recent star of the movie *Shrek 2*

Rita
Sassy cat in *Animaniacs* TV cartoons; sidekick of Runt, a dog

Rum Tum Tugger
Rakish tomcat in *Cats*

Shere Khan
Tiger in Kipling's *The Jungle Book*

Stimpy
Fat cat in *Ren & Stimpy* TV cartoons

That Darn Cat
A Disney movie star

The Cat in the Hat
Dr. Seuss's famous feline with a red-and-white-banded stovepipe hat

Three Little Kittens
They lost their mittens. Awww!

Tigger
Bouncy tiger in Winnie the Pooh stories

Tom
Jerry's co-star in Hanna-Barbera's cartoons

Toonces
Car-driving cat in *Saturday Night Live* sketches

Top Cat
Star of a Hanna-Barbera animated prime-time series on ABC

Yum-Yum
The other Siamese cat in Lilian Jackson Braun mysteries